Note how a church operates
"by faith"

A. Staffing

B. finances

C. Services

Pastor Calvin L. Bodeutsch
5 Chapel Place
Wayne, N. J.   07470

HOPE FOR YOUR CHURCH

TEN PRINCIPLES OF CHURCH GROWTH

by Harold L. Fickett, Jr.

G/L
REGAL
BOOKS
TM

A Division of G/L Publications
Glendale, California, U.S.A.

Photo credits: Page 35 (bottom): Frank Moody.
All other photos: David J. Pavol.

Other Regal books by Dr. Fickett:
JAMES: Faith That Works
Baptist Beliefs

Second Edition

Published by
Regal Books Division, G/L Publications
Glendale, California 91209, U.S.A.

Library of Congress Catalog Card No. 72-94164
ISBN 0-8307-0207-5

Contents

A Word About This Book

A Word About This Book

Dr. Wilbur M. Smith writes of the First Baptist Church of Van Nuys, California, that "the moment one enters the sanctuary he is aware of the pulse of its spiritual life. Its phenomenal attendance at all services and its innumerable activities are the result of a Bible-centered ministry and a congregation rejoicing in work for the Lord."

I, too, have had the privilege of visiting the church from time to time and sensing the presence of God in a most unusual way. The challenge and blessing of the message and program remind us of the first century church about which we are told that "more and more believers were added to the Lord, crowds both of men and women."

This book is not only the story of the Van Nuys Baptist Church, but a practical handbook on church growth. Many pastors and people are discouraged today and when asked about their work take refuge in a false assumption that all churches are experiencing decline. Any church of any size anywhere that will put into practice these principles of growth can experience the abundant blessing of God. The Van Nuys story is not first a matter of culture or area or a man but a practical plan with primary emphasis on the Word of God and with total dependence upon the Holy Spirit.

If you are looking for practical ideas, suggestions, and a basic plan of church growth, this book will be of inestimable help. The late Dr. Henrietta C. Mears always stressed the importance of a plan in the Lord's work. "If man wants to build a place for a large business, he doesn't phone the cement company and have bags of cement piled on his lot, or phone the lumber company and have stacks of lumber piled everywhere. He doesn't start to order the materials until he has a plan."

What plan do you have for your church? What principles and specifications are you following?

A plan is essential in building a church. Furthermore, a man is called to lead in the execution of a plan. When God has a job to do He places His hand upon a man. By faith and work that man experiences the wisdom and power of the Holy Spirit. You may think that your church has little potential, that it is too small to experience great things. Remember, Dr. Fickett started in obscurity and with smallness. The Van Nuys church started with fifteen members that met in an old railroad car parked on a siding. Your job is not to build a large church but a great church to the glory of God, regardless of size, to draw together in fellowship a company of spiritually minded believers who care for others, whose hearts overflow with love for each other, and the lost and needy.

Dr. W. A. Criswell, pastor of the great First Baptist Church of Dallas, Texas writes, "There is no minister of the gospel in the earth who has done a greater work for God in building a church than Dr. Harold L. Fickett, pastor of the Van Nuys Baptist Church. There are no difficulties too hard or too complex for him to face boldly and vigorously and with ultimate triumph. He has set a pattern for us of which he himself is a paragon by which every pastor can measure his work and learn how to do it more successfully.

May God gloriously bless to the use of thousands of our ministers and laymen this volume *Hope for Your Church* in which Dr. Fickett has shared his tested "Ten Principles of Church Growth."

Cyrus N. Nelson

President, Gospel Light Publications

Introduction

In 1914 the First Baptist Church of Van Nuys was organized with fifteen charter members. Their original meeting place was an old railroad car parked on an outmoded siding in the southern part of the little village of Van Nuys. The history of this church reveals that the members who initiated the program had great vision. They believed that God would use them to develop a Christ-centered institution that would have a profound impact upon the entire area of Southern California.

During the nearly 57 years that have ensued since that time, the Almighty has seen fit to bless the church. At the present, the First Baptist Church of Van Nuys occupies 21 acres of property in the very heart of the San Fernando Valley, at the corner of Sherman Way and Kester.

A recent appraisal of the church property reveals that it is now valued at something over $6 million. In addition to the property in Van Nuys the church also has four campsites: one in Lake Arrowhead, one in

Malibu, one in Frazier Park and one in Baja, California. Present membership of the church is just a little more than 9,300. And the budget for this year is $1.5 million.

During the past twelve years there has not been a Sunday gone by without at least one person making a decision for Christ and the church. During this same period of time the church has had a baptismal service every Sunday night, with the exception of about eight or nine times, when there have been candidates for baptism, but the programs precluded such a service.

There is no doubt about the fact that the Spirit of God is controlling, blessing and leading this church. As we think about all of this the question naturally arises, why has the Almighty seen fit to place His imprimatur upon this church in such a special way. As one who has served as its pastor for twelve years I have thought much about this. I am convinced that there are ten basic reasons which I would like to discuss with you in the following chapters.

CHAPTER 1

Christ Centered

God is blessing us because we are a Christ-centered institution. We have the same attitude as the apostle Paul which he expressed in Colossians 1:18 *that He Himself might come to have first place in everything.* We take the same position concerning our program as Billy Graham does toward his. You have heard him say many times from public platforms, and over radio and on television, "If the Lord were to take His hand off of my ministry, the world would write Ichabod over everything I say and do." The Psalmist expressed our philosophy in Psalm 127:1 when he wrote: *Unless the Lord builds the house, They labor in vain who build it;* unless the Lord builds the church, they labor in vain that build it.

In any evangelical church there is a place for only one Mr. Big, only one dictator and that only one is

1

Jesus Christ. In our church we will not tolerate personal empire builders. Through the years that I have been here, there have been several who have attempted to be such. They have looked upon themselves as eminently qualified lay leaders. They have wanted to dictate the policies that are carried out by our various organizations. In each situation our people have reacted wonderfully. Whenever these individuals have had good suggestions our members have willingly and enthusiastically implemented them. Whenever the suggestions have not been too good—and most of the time this has been the case—they reacted not by fighting back, but by letting them go in one ear and out the other. In each case it has not been long until the individual has seen the handwriting on the wall and has been convinced that his services and talents might be more appreciated somewhere else. Consequently, through these years we have experienced several backdoor revivals and blessed deletions.

This reminds me of the story of the pastor who said that he put on a membership drive in his church and drove out fifteen. Whenever an individual wants to put himself in the position of being the church dictator, the best thing that can happen is for that individual to go. I learned this when I was just a little boy.

My father was the pastor of the Mount Washington Baptist Church in Kansas City, Missouri. One Sunday morning after he had finished preaching a sermon on tithing, the Chairman of the Board of Deacons, who looked upon himself as the lay leader of the church, stood in the back of the sanctuary and denounced the message. He told the people that it was not necessary for them to pay any attention to what the pastor had said—that the sermon was not based on biblical truth. He contended that tithing was neither required nor expected of the Christian—that, as far as supporting the

The cross of the Lord Jesus Christ is at the center of the message of the First Baptist Church of Van Nuys.

church was concerned, all that the believer needed to do was to give as he saw fit.

My dad had just come into the ministry from a business, and he did not handle this matter with a soft touch. He did not look upon it as something that needed to be treated with diplomacy. Instead, he called a business meeting of the church which resulted in the hand of fellowship being withdrawn from this deacon. The deacon left, and 90 of his followers went with him. They organized a new church in a nearby community which lasted for only about five years. Their sanctuary was sold to a garage, and they were out of business.

Just as soon as the Mount Washington Baptist Church had that backdoor revival, the Spirit of God began to bless it as it had never been blessed before. Phenomenal growth took place. New property was added to the church. New buildings were constructed. People were saved at all the services. Young men and young women went to the mission fields and into the ministry, and the program was tremendously vital in meeting the needs of all the people. By getting rid of that would-be church dictator and his followers, that church experienced both revival and expansion. Remember, there is a place for only one Mr. Big in any evangelical church and that One is none other than the King of kings and Lord of lords, Jesus Christ, our only sufficient Saviour.

CHAPTER 2

Biblically Based

God is blessing our church because the Bible is our textbook. It is preached from our pulpit and taught in our Sunday school. We take the position that the Bible does not contain the Word of God—it is the Word of God. It is therefore our high privilege as well as our great responsibility to share its inspired and sacred truths with all who come within our doors. In this connection, one of the things that greatly troubles me when I am with my fellow ministers and we are talking about preaching, inevitably one of them will say that it is our job to make the Bible relevant to our contemporaries. If I thought this was my task, I would get out of the ministry; for I cannot make the Bible relevant to anyone. I am not that intelligent. But thank God I don't have to be, for the Bible *is* relevant in meeting the needs of people. My responsibility is to

7

study it in depth, to pray over it, to ask the Spirit of God to fill me with its revelation and then to stand in the pulpit and preach the message that the Almighty has laid upon my heart. When I do this, I have no problem with relevancy. The Spirit of God takes what I say and makes it meaningful to those who are listening to me.

Yes, the Bible which is relevant in meeting the needs of modern man is the textbook of our church. This does not mean that we do not use Sunday school literature; we do. But we insist that our instructors teach from the Bible. We tell them that literature is simply an aid in understanding the text. If the literature that we furnish them does not give them enough assistance, we encourage them to go to our library and use its facilities. We want them to be thoroughly familiar with the text which they are going to teach. Then when they stand before their class, they leave the commentaries and the literature behind and take with them only the Word of God. Sunday school literature is important, but only as a means to an end, not an end in itself. And, by the way, are you aware that there are three ways in which a church can easily be destroyed?

The first is by getting it to fight over its denominational affiliation. The second is by inciting it to fight over its Sunday school curriculum. The third is by having the pastor run away with the deacon's wife. This third way, however, is not nearly as devastating as the other two, because when it occurs, inevitably the people will say that the pastor was of the flesh, and will seek a replacement. However, when they get to fighting either over the denomination affiliation or over Sunday school literature they really get angry and oftentimes it takes years to heal the wounds that result from the conflict. Such activity is devastating to the body of Christ.

"I am convinced that wherever the Bible is preached, church growth comes naturally," states Pastor Fickett.

Shortly after becoming pastor of the First Baptist Church in Van Nuys I discovered that they had just gone through a donnybrook over the Sunday school literature. This resulted in their deciding upon a definite curriculum. As I viewed the situation, there were some changes that I wanted to make in that curriculum. I did not do this, however, because I was convinced that this would only add fuel to the embers of the old fire. Instead, I simply supplemented where I felt that supplementation would help the situation. And God saw fit to bless this strategy. I would recommend to churches having problems in this area, that they profit by our experience. In so doing they will have peace instead of war.

People today are hungry for the Word of God. They want preachers and teachers who have a vision from the Lord that they can share with them. Whenever the church has a Bible preaching and teaching ministry, the people will come. Growth is inevitable.

Several months ago I was asked, along with Bishop Gerald Kennedy of the Methodist Church, to represent Word Publications Company in a press conference here in Los Angeles. We were being interviewed by the press, by radio and television commentators concerning our attitude toward the Children's New Testament that had recently been published by Word. In the course of the interview, one commentator deviated from the subject and asked, "Is church attendance increasing or decreasing?"

Bishop Kennedy responded immediately, "It is decreasing—definitely on the decline."

The commentator looked at me and inquired, "What do you think?"

"It all depends," I replied.

Bishop Kennedy very politely said, "May I interrupt?"

10

I answered, "You're the Bishop. Go right ahead."

He then made this very provocative and true statement: "You're right. Wherever the Bible is preached and Christ is exalted, church growth naturally comes. Attendance in churches like this today is on the increase."

CHAPTER 3

Evangelistic

God is blessing our church because we are evangelistic. We are committed to the idea that men and women need to know Christ in a personal viable way.

Back in the 1950s, Dr. D. T. Niles wrote a book entitled *The Preacher's Task—The Stone of Stumbling.* This book is his Lyman Beecher lectures on preaching which he delivered at Yale Divinity School two or three years before.

In this volume, Dr. Niles takes the position that it is not the task of the church to go out and tell people that they need to know Christ. Rather, it is the responsibility of God's servants to share with the various peoples of the world that they are already saved—that all they need to do is recognize it. This is a subtle form of universalism which in my opinion is antithetical to the teaching of the Scripture and is devastating to the life of the church that adopts it.

Long ago the wisest man who ever lived, Solomon, wrote in Proverbs 11:30, *The fruit of the righteous is a tree of life, And he who is wise wins souls . . .*

Several years ago in the city of Philadelphia I had the privilege of having lunch with Dr. William Mueller, the distinguished professor of Church History at the New Orleans Baptist Theological Seminary in New Orleans, Louisiana. In the course of our conversation he told me the delightful story of a monastery in his native Germany. This particular monastery trained Christian brothers for various responsibilities within the Roman Catholic Church. He said that there was one Christian brother in training who lived in mortal fear of being called upon to preach the sermon in the daily chapel exercises. As this young man thought about his apprehension he decided to head it off by going to the Monitor of the monastery and discussing the problem with him. In the course of the conversation he said, "Sir, I am willing to do any menial job that you assign me. I would be delighted to go out into the fields and plow them, fertilize and irrigate them by hand to increase their productivity. If you would care for me to do so, I would be happy to get down on my hands and knees and scrub the floors here in the monastery. It would be a privilege for me to polish the silverware. Any menial job that you call upon me to do I shall be happy to do. However, please don't ask me to preach a sermon in the chapel."

The Monitor, looking at the young man and recognizing that an assignment to preach was exactly what he needed, replied, "Tomorrow you are to conduct the chapel and preach the sermon." The next day as this young brother stood behind the pulpit and looked out into the eyes of his peers who had assembled in the sanctuary, he was greatly apprehensive. He was so nervous he hardly knew what to do. He started his sermon by asking, "Brothers, do you know what I am going to say?" They all shook their heads in the negative. He continued, "Neither do I. Let's stand for the benediction. Pax vobiscum."

Naturally, the Monitor was infuriated by this. He said to the young man, "I am going to give you a second chance. Tomorrow you are to conduct the service in the chapel, and this time I want you to preach a message."

The next day the scene was the same. And the young man began as he had the day before, "Brothers, do you know what I am going to say?" When they all nodded their heads in the affirmative, he said, "Since you already know, there is no point in my saying it. Let's stand for the benediction. Pax vobiscum."

The Monitor was livid with anger. Once again he went to the young brother and literally roared at him, "I am tired of your chicanery. Tomorrow I am going to give you a third chance. If you don't come through, I am going to put you in solitary confinement on bread and water."

The third day the scene was the same. The brother began as he had the two previous days, "Brothers, do you know what I am going to say?" Some nodded their heads in the affirmative. Some shook their heads in the negative. He then said, "Let those who know tell those who don't. Let's stand for the benediction. Pax vobiscum."

"Let those who know tell those who don't." This is an abbreviated form of the great commission. Our Lord Jesus Christ expects those of us who are Christians to share our faith in Christ with others; He demands that we be evangelistic.

The membership of the First Baptist Church of Van Nuys ascribes to the idea that this is our number one responsibility. Ours therefore is a witnessing church. Every phase of our program has but one purpose in it, and that is to reach people for Jesus Christ and build them up in the faith.

During the twelve years that I have been pastor of this church Campus Crusade has conducted four Laymen's Institutes for Evangelism for us. We have trained more than 1,400 workers in the art of sharing their faith in Jesus Christ with those who do not know Him. This has been one of the most fruitful things that we have done. I recommend to any evangelical church that is really concerned about winning people to the Saviour to follow this plan. Campus Crusade for Christ through these Laymen's Institutes really knows how to turn on men and women for the Saviour. Let me give you just one example.

In our last Institute our Lay Chairman was a brilliant young lawyer. After the training had been completed and we were giving testimonies as to the blessing each one of us had received from it, this attorney said something like this: "All of my life as a Christian I have known that I should share my faith with others. Prior to taking this Laymen's Institute for Evangelism course, however, I was convinced that in approaching someone else about the gospel I had to bring up all the intellectual arguments concerning the veracity of the Scriptures. I discovered that each time I did this inevitably the person to whom I was witnessing had a contrary opinion. Instead of winning him to the Saviour I found myself in an argument with him. Yesterday when we went out on cold turkey evangelism I simply read the four spiritual laws to the people to whom I was speaking. After reading the laws I asked them if they would like to pray the prayer to receive Christ. Within less than two hours five people had made their decisions for the Saviour. Even though this may be a very simple plan I am convinced that the Holy Spirit brought it into being and blesses the person who uses it. Therefore, until a better plan is devised, I am going to continue doing this."

This young lawyer has done exactly what he said he would do. At the present time he is the best personal soul winner among lay people that I know anything about. For example, in one week he had five couples come to him wanting him to help them get a divorce. In each of the situations he won both the husband and the wife to Christ, and they were reconciled in the Saviour to one another. Instead of their homes ending in divorce they are now Christ-centered institutions. Laughingly he told me, "If I keep this up, it won't be long until I will put myself out of business."

As the result of this same Laymen's Institute for Evangelism, Don a young machinist in our church who had accepted Christ just six months before was really turned on for the Saviour. Since that time he has literally been on fire to share his faith with everyone with whom he comes in contact.

Just recently we have had our former pastor, my predecessor, Dr. Porter L. Barrington, lead us in a nine-day "Witness With Confidence Crusade." His teaching is based upon *The Christian Life New Testament*, which he has edited. The approach which he uses is like a post-graduate course to the training offered by the Laymen's Institute for Evangelism. The two fit together like a hand in a glove. In this crusade more than 1,200 persons took the course, and over 1,000 signed commitment cards indicating their decisions to work faithfully in the church's witnessing program. As pastor, I want you to know that when these results were tabulated and announced I was on shouting ground. I found myself singing the doxology with every fiber of my being.

About six months ago we began a bus ministry. Don volunteered to be one of our drivers. Within two months he had built up a route to such an extent that it was necessary for us to split it into two. Later he decided that God would have him visit the families of all the children who rode his bus. He had the courage to implement this decision. The first family on which he called was that of a Mexican-American couple who had eight children. As he began to talk to the parents about Jesus Christ, he discovered that the father was quite knowledgeable as far as the content of the Bible was concerned. He and his brother-in-law, who was visiting in the home, began to ply Don with questions concerning the Scripture. It wasn't long until Don was completely over his head and unable to handle the situation. Finally, in desperation he said to these two men and the wife, "I am a Baptist bus driver. I am not a theologian. I love Jesus Christ. Even though I can't answer all of your theological questions, I would like to share with you the four spiritual laws." He then proceeded to deal with them on the basis of this Campus Crusade technique in witnessing. When he had finished, he asked the father, the mother and the brother-in-law if they would like to pray to receive Christ in their lives. When they answered in the affirmative, Don led them in the prayer in which they invited the Lord to come into their hearts and take over. The father and mother rejoiced in this decision.

Immediately they became concerned about their eight children. Without anyone telling them to do so, they began a family altar around the dinner table each night. The father would read a passage of Scripture and then ask the children to explain what it meant. In the course of these discussions centered around the Word of God, the parents led all eight of their children to the Saviour. I have had the privilege of baptizing this entire family. The father now is really turned on for Christ and is doing exactly what Don did. He is sharing his faith with all with whom he comes in contact.

Not too long ago one of his friends from Mexico, a teenage boy, was visiting in his home. The father led this boy to Jesus Christ. He brought him to our church. Even though the lad did not understand any English, when the invitation was given he came forward to make a public confession of his faith in the Saviour. I had the privilege of baptizing him. I predict that this is going to be a chain reaction—that many are going to come to know Christ as their Saviour and Lord through the activity that was started by Don who literally spends all of his spare time in presenting the Saviour to others.

Whenever I get up to preach on Sunday morning or Sunday night I know that someone will be coming forward when the invitation is given. The reason for this is not that I am a profound thinker, an erudite scholar, a scintillating speaker or a prince of pulpiteers. This knowledge is based upon the fact that our lay workers who have been trained in evangelism have been sharing their faith with others during the week. The Spirit of God has crowned the efforts of many of these with success. Consequently, they have been able to win those with whom they have shared their faith to a saving knowledge of Jesus Christ. Inevitably they will have these, whom they have won in the services with them, prepared to make their public decisions just as soon as the invitation is given.

Yes, our church is an evangelistic church. Every facet of our program is geared with one purpose in mind, that of reaching others with the Good News of Jesus Christ.

We have a great music program. At the present time

there are 35 choirs with more than 1,600 people taking part. Through this medium we have been able to win a number of people to the Saviour and have developed outreaches that are almost unbelievable in what they have been able to accomplish for Christ.

For example, about four years ago my minister of music, Dr. John Gustafson, and I were playing golf down at Palm Springs. He said to me, "Preacher, we should do something about the college kids that come down here during the pre-Easter week simply to raise cain and have a good time. No one is seeking to win these people to Jesus. There is no evangelistic program to challenge them. I believe that our church should develop one." To this I readily agreed.

When we went home we met with our Minister of Education, Mr. Lowell Brown, and talked the matter over. As a result of this we organized what is known now as "the Certain Sounds." This is a musical organization composed of 12 singers and 12 instrumentalists. Their music is basically folk rock. Through the years these young people developed into a real professional group. We trained other workers in the Campus Crusade techniques in winning people to Christ. As a matter of fact that first year, which is now several years ago, 100 of the sharpest, most turned on kids I have ever known took this training. They were really ready for the initial invasion of Palm Springs.

But we had a problem. We did not know where we were going to conduct this program. Consequently, John, Lowell and I went down to Palm Springs seeking the most advantageous location. As we looked around the city we were convinced that the logical place was the Chi Chi Night Club, on the main drag.

We contacted the business manager and told him that we would like to rent the club during the pre-Easter Week. He responded by saying that they had recently spent over $20,000 in refurbishing the place. They were not interested in renting it; they wanted to sell it.

I said, "Suppose you don't sell it? Will you let us lease it for that week?"

He asked me, "For what do you want to use it?"

I replied, "For an evangelistic program that will go something like this: during the afternoons in the bar area we will have free food and soft drinks for all the kids who want to come in and take advantage of this opportunity. We will provide small entertainment either with a guitarist or maybe a duet or a trio.

"Seated at each of the tables in that area will be one of our personal workers. After the kids get their sandwiches and drinks they will sit at the tables and listen to this entertainment. While so doing, our workers will begin to talk to them about Jesus Christ. In the course of the conversation they will seek to lead these kids to the place where they will invite the Saviour into their lives. In the evening we will use the ballroom area for a program by our Certain Sounds which will be basically folk rock music interspersed with Christian testimonies. After the program our personal workers, who have been mingling with the crowd, begin to talk to the people about what Jesus can do for them." And then I added, "If you will let us do this, I will guarantee that this will be the best purpose for which the Chi Chi has ever been used."

I could see that this readily appealed to this business man. I was therefore not surprised when he said, "We will let you use it, providing we don't sell it before Easter."

I inquired, "How much will it cost us?"

He answered, "Just $8.00 to turn on the lights."

After assuring him that we could raise that amount

of money, I said, "We are going to pray that you don't sell it."

When he replied, "That's not fair," I said laughingly, "Well, then, we will pray that you don't sell it until after Easter; then it will be all right."

He didn't sell it, and we moved in with our program. In so doing, we found that instead of having one concert in the ballroom each night we had to put on four in order to accommodate the crowds. As the result of that week, more than 200 young people invited Jesus Christ to become their Saviour and Lord.

We followed up those who made decisions by sending them literature designed to help them in their Christian life. We also contacted the evangelical churches in the area in which they lived, encouraging them to enlist these converts in their activities.

The policemen told us that we had cut the crime rate in Palm Springs by 60%. The cops themselves became so pleased with what we accomplished that they took up an offering and out of their own pockets they collected $100.00. I laughingly told the lieutenant who gave us the money that all of my life I had contributed to the police force, but that this was the first time they had ever given anything to me except parking tickets.

The City Council in Palm Springs invited us that year to make this an annual pilgrimage. This we have done. Unfortunately, the Chi Chi Night Club was sold, but the city fathers have provided for us the only open lot in the downtown area.

Each year before the Easter Week our boys go down and construct a plywood fence around this lot and erect a stage. They paint it psychedelic and we call it "The Gate." Here, night after night, the concerts are presented to capacity audiences. In addition to The Gate we also have a coffeehouse in which we minister to the kids throughout the day.

The musical program including the church choir and The
Certain Sounds has pointed thousands of people to Christ.

After our first experience in Palm Springs our young people were so enamored with the opportunity of serving Christ in this way, that they decided to devote Fourth of July weekend to an invasion of Catalina Island with the same program. We were able to lease an old destroyer on which to ship our goods and to transport our personnel. The civic leaders of Avalon looked rather skeptically at what we were doing and refused to let the ship come to the dock. We, therefore, had to unload it in small boats. This was a most difficult chore. Nevertheless our young gang was up to it and performed yeoman service in accomplishing the feat.

While we were in Avalon, however, the same civic leaders changed their attitude towards us. After the first concert they were really convinced that we had something which they needed.

One incident that took place that first year illustrates the power of this type of evangelism. During one of the concerts a gang of typical hoods suddenly appeared. They were dressed in black pants with boots, big black belts and leather jackets. It appeared as if they were going to try to destroy the concert. Some of our fellows that were with us in the personal workers team were college football players. When they saw this situation they knew something had to be done. They approached the gang, and John, one of our fellows, said to the leader of the gang, "What do you guys want?"

Our man was 6 feet 2 inches and weighed 215 pounds. Their leader was a little scrawny guy about 5 feet 7 inches. He looked up and said, "I am going to beat the hell out of you and then we are going to break up this concert."

John, peering down at him, replied, "You are going to do what?"

He repeated, "I am going to beat the hell out of you and then we are going to break up this concert."

The Spirit of God really helped John at this point. He said, "Well, if you have the guts to try to beat me up, you at least ought to have the guts to listen to what I have to say."

The leader agreed, "That's a fair deal."

John went on, "Don't you know that God loves you and has a wonderful plan for your life? But sin has made you a slave and you are separated from God. He has done something about this. He sent His only Son Jesus Christ to die on Calvary and then conquered death in order that He might provide a way by which you can be saved. What you really need to do right now is get down on your knees and ask Jesus Christ to come into your life. If you will, I will guarantee you that He will free you from sin—that you will be completely changed. You will find something really worth living for."

The young hood shook his head and said, "I'll have to think this over." So with his gang he left.

About one hour and a half later he came back looking for John. When he found him he said, "Man, you have something that I need. How can I get it?"

Our big old football player put his arm around this little leader of that gang of hoods, and suggested, "Let's get right down on our knees and ask Christ to forgive your sins and then you ask Him to come into your life."

The gang leader queried. "Right here in front of all these people?

"Yes, right here in front of all these people."

That hood did exactly what he was told. He got down on his knees. He asked God to forgive him of his sins and he invited Christ to come into his heart. Instead of those hoods breaking up the concert, the leader found Christ and immediately began to share his faith with the others in his gang.

Before this experience on the Fourth of July weekend had been terminated, the city fathers in Avalon were so grateful for what we had done, they invited us to come back during the Labor Day weekend in September. We explained to them that our financial resources had come to an end. We just didn't have the funds with which to do that. They responded, "We will take care of the expense. We can use tax money to bring you over again. It will save us financially in the long run, because we won't have to hire nearly so many off duty policemen when you are here. We have found that you have perceptively cut our crime rate during this weekend." So each year since that time, we have gone to Avalon with this approach, and the Lord has blessed us.

In 1968 we decided to send the Certain Sounds to the Orient for a missionary tour. That summer they had the privilege of being in Japan, Taiwan, the Philippines and Hong Kong. While their ministry had been effective on this tour, at the end of the summer as we began to appraise the situation we decided that there was something missing—that we needed someone or some group of people to prepare for the coming of the Certain Sounds and then do the follow-up work after they left. Therefore, the next two summers we sent what we called the Missionary Assistance Corps to help at these two points. In 1969 there were forty of the MAC who preceded the Certain Sounds and set up their concerts. They then remained in the area and did the follow-up work after the Certain Sounds had presented their message in song.

In 1970 we actually sent sixty MAC personnel. This combination of the Sounds and the Missionary Assistance Corps was far more effective in getting the job done than the Certain Sounds were by themselves. They are excellent musicians. As a matter of fact, they are so good that they have an open invitation right now to sing on national television in Japan, Taiwan and in the Philippines. However, their entire ministry was centered around music. They didn't have any time to follow up afterwards. The Missionary Assistance Corps, however, did and as a result there were many people who came to know Jesus Christ as Saviour and Lord in a personal way.

Let me document this for you. In 1969, after the Certain Sounds had presented a concert at one of the universities in the Philippines, a woman whom we will call Mrs. L asked two of our Missionary Assistance Corps girls to come to her apartment. Shortly after arriving and exchanging the amenities of the day, Mrs. L said to them, "I want to know how I can experience salvation through Jesus Christ." Our two girls took her through the four spiritual laws. They prayed with her about accepting Christ as Saviour, and as a result she had a wonderful conversion experience.

Mrs. L is the principal of the largest high school in Manila. After she was converted she invited our Missionary Assistance Corps personnel to come into her high school on a given day and go from classroom to classroom, explaining to all of the students how they could come to know Jesus Christ personally. The entire day was given to the evangelization of the student body because their principal, as the result of a combination ministry of the Certain Sounds and the Missionary Assistance Corps, had made her decision for Jesus Christ.

Last year our Certain Sounds were invited to sing at the West Point of the Philippines. This institution is located in Baguio, the summer capitol. The student body is made up of 400 young men who are the sharpest to be found anywhere in the Philippine Islands. They are handpicked for this particular school. Our Certain Sounds is the only Christian group that has ever been invited to perform there. Their invitation was based on their promise not to sing any Christian music. However, in making that promise they persuaded the commandant of the school to agree that they could say whatever they cared to between numbers. From the school's standpoint that is where they made their mistake. The Certain Sounds turned the cadets on with their music. Between numbers they gave their testimonies for Christ. When the concert was concluded, the students who wanted to know more about Jesus Christ were invited to sign up for Bible correspondence courses. Two hundred responded to this invitation. This meant that 50% of that entire student body, as a result of this concert and the testimonies, decided that they needed to know more about the Saviour.

We left a small group of our Missionary Assistance Corps to work with these 200 on that campus. During the remaining weeks of the summer these MAC people were able to win most of the 200 personally to a saving knowledge of Jesus Christ. When they left the campus the new converts were meeting in small groups for prayer, Bible study and strategy planning as to how they could reach the other cadets as well as their faculty for Christ.

This musical program has really resulted in pointing literally thousands of people to Jesus Christ as Saviour and Lord. Not only do we use our musical program for this purpose but we use every other church activity to achieve the same goal. Let me give you a "for instance."

Five years ago we found that the Little Leagues were playing on Sunday here in the San Fernando Valley. I recognized that it would do me very little good to stand in the pulpit and cry out against this desecration of the Lord's day. I knew that those who were in charge would just laugh at me and go merrily on their way doing exactly what they pleased. Instead of fighting it publicly we decided to offer our people an alternative. We began a Little League Baseball Program that summer in our own church. And then we extended it to Little League Football and finally to Little League Basketball. Each year now, we have these three Little League Programs taking place in our church. Three to four hundred boys are participating in them. Most of them are not actually related directly to our church. They come from the neighborhood, and they have various backgrounds. Many of them have never known who Jesus Christ actually is.

At the end of each of these seasons we have a hamburger fry for the boys with their dads in our gymnasium. At this time we give a trophy to every boy who has played on a team. There are no exceptions; all are included. The only difference we make between the winners and the losers is the size of the trophy. This creates a very congenial atmosphere in which happiness prevails. The program is concluded on each of these occasions with some outstanding sports figure presenting the gospel and then inviting those present to receive Jesus Christ as Saviour and Lord. The results have been most gratifying.

I am convinced that any church, regardless of its size, can put on a similar program. In every community there are hundreds and hundreds of boys that are not related to any church, but who are interested in athletics. If a church will take advantage of this by enabling these boys to participate in the sports they enjoy, the boys will readily accept that opportunity. And then they will be all ears when the message of Christ is presented to them.

In our San Fernando Valley we have a number of rest homes. We have found that these present to us a great opportunity for sharing our faith with those who are in desperate need. As we have examined these rest homes, we have discovered that most of the people in them have been placed there by relatives who (basically) have just wanted to get them off of their hands. After they put their aged ones into these institutions, they very seldom visit them. Consequently these are very very lonely people. Recognizing all of this, several years ago we organized what we call our Project Cheer program.

This particular outreach is made up of a number of evangelistic teams organized within our Sunday school to go out on Sunday afternoons to conduct services in the rest homes that are open to us. We have discovered that these services are really appreciated by those that are living in the homes.

I remember several years ago my son led a junior high school group which participated in this project. In talking to his mother about it he said, "Mom we just sing and give our testimony and then I preach to those older people just as if they were kids. And they love it." Then he shared with us an experience which he had had. He said, "One Sunday afternoon after I had finished preaching, a dear old lady asked me to come to her bedside. When I walked over to where she was, she said, 'Please kneel down.' As I did, she took both of my cheeks in her two hands and, drawing me close to her, she begged, 'Let me look into your young eyes. I haven't seen a young person in so long it is just honey to my soul to be able to see you." And then he added, "Tears were streaming down her cheeks."

Sunday after Sunday our Project Cheer teams go into these homes. They dispense cheer to those who are already Christians. They share their faith in Christ with those who are not, and this has resulted and continues to result in many personal decisions for Jesus Christ. And just think of this! Those people are not long for this world. If they die without Christ they have no hope. They are destined to be eternally separated from God. Our Project Cheer people realizing the truth of this are faithfully going Sunday after Sunday into these rest homes in order that they might help these aged people prepare for that which lies ahead of them in eternity. I am thankful for all who have found Christ as a result of this outreach. Many of them have departed this life and are now personally with our blessed Lord.

Yes, our church is an evangelistic church. In this connection one of the things that is greatly encouraged to me as the pastor is the fact that many of our families, yes, I would say most of our families, are concerned about winning the lost to Jesus Christ. They take advantage of every opportunity presented to them to introduce others to the Saviour. Let me give you a case in point.

Bud, a 45-year-old member of our church, was in a brick yard in Sepulveda to pick up some material with which to do a job at home. While looking around the yard, a cement truck backed up over him. He was taken to the hospital where he died while on the operating table. Just as soon as I heard about this, I made my way to the hospital as fast as I could get there in order to be with his lovely wife, Lou. By the time I arrived he had been dead for about five minutes. I found that Lou was taking advantage of this opportunity to share her faith in Christ with all who would listen to her. As I walked with her out of the hospital, a doctor very kindly inquired, "Can I help you by giving you a sedative?"

Her sister Carolyn, who was walking on the other side of her, answered, "Doctor, my sister doesn't need

31

any sedative. She has Jesus Christ. The Master will meet her needs."

I escorted Lou back to her home. As we sat in the living room talking about the funeral service she said, "Pastor, I want you to preach the gospel in such a straightforward manner that everyone there will know how he or she can be saved." I promised her that I would do that.

Just before the service Lou called a number of her friends who were not Christians and to each one of them she said something like this, "I am calling to invite you to attend Bud's funeral. Through the years that you and I have been friends I have tried to get you to come to our church. Thus far I have not been successful. However, in this time of sorrow I need you. I trust that you will be in the sanctuary for the service." Everyone of these people were there. I had the opportunity of preaching the gospel to them and as a result of this souls were saved.

And there is another part of this story that is quite intriguing. Lou and Bud have a teenage son, Allan, who feels called to the ministry. As he talked to his mother concerning the family situation, he said words to this effect, "Mother, as I think about Dad's death, I am reminded of the story of the three shepherds who were living in a barren region. They wanted to find pasture for their sheep. They mounted their horses and began to search for it. Finally they came upon a river. A voice said to them, 'Dismount; let your horses drink from the river, and you wade out into the stream and pick up rocks.' These shepherds, although they were tough and hard, were obedient to the voice. They picked up rocks and filled their pockets with them. As they stood in the stream the voice once again said to them, 'Go back and mount your horses. Ride for an hour into the desert, then dismount and sleep there for the night. In the morning when you awaken you will be both sad and glad.' They were obedient to that voice. The next morning when they awakened they found that the rocks which they had picked up had been turned into diamonds. They were sad because they had not picked up more rocks. They were glad, however, about the transformation of the rocks which they had put into their pockets."

After telling this story Allan said, "Mother, that's the way it is with us. God has had us bend over and pick up a rather heavy rock in the death of daddy. We are going to miss him. Even though we know he is with the Lord and we have nothing to fear as far as his future is concerned, we still are going to miss him. However, mother, out of this rock God is going to fashion many diamonds."

Later on when I was talking to Allan about this story I asked him, "Did you mean by this, Allan, that because all of you are Christians, God will see to it that eventually you will be together again in that celestial city which the Bible calls heaven? Is that the diamond that God is going to make out of the rock?"

He responded, "Yes, Pastor, that is one of the diamonds. But I believe that He is going to form many others. As a matter of fact He has already produced one." He then said, "You know Faye in our Church?" I assured him that I did. He went on, "When Faye heard that my daddy had passed away she went to her mother who was sick in bed and said, 'Allan has great assurance that even though his dad is dead everything is all right. If anything happened to you, mother, I would want that same assurance. However, I couldn't have it because you are not a Christian. If you were to die right now, instead of going to heaven you would spend eternity in hell. Just the thought of this breaks my heart. Mother, won't you accept Jesus Christ as your

Saviour and Lord this very moment?' And the mother said, 'Yes, Faye, I will.' " Then Allan looked at me and asked, "Isn't it wonderful, Pastor, that God has already given us a diamond out of this rock?"

In my pulpit ministry I am evangelistic. This is not to say that I do not believe in teaching. I definitely do. As a matter of fact most of my messages are expositions of the Scriptures; the didactic element is very much a part of my preaching. However, I am convinced that no sermon is worth its salt unless it is redemptive. At every one of our services the plan of salvation is presented and people are invited to acknowledge Christ, whom to know aright is life—life abundant here and now, and life everlasting.

Laymen learn to share Christ with others at work. The bus ministry brings hundreds of kids to hear the gospel.

CHAPTER 4

A Regenerated Membership

God is blessing our Church because we do our utmost to have a regenerate church membership. More than twenty years ago, Canon Green, the famous Anglican visited the United States. After being in our churches for a number of months, he returned to his native England. When he was interviewed by the British press as to his impressions of church life in our country, he made a statement that has stayed with me all these years. He said, "I am convinced that the most fertile field for evangelism in America is among the unconverted church members in that land."

If you were to ask me what I think is the greatest problem churches face today, without a moment's hesitation I would answer, "It is the problem of our unconverted church members." I have thought much about this and meditated upon it. I feel that I have the answer as to why this situation actually exists. I have the conviction that many people join a church today simply because they are enamored with a particular pastor rather than having fallen in love with Jesus Christ. When that pastor resigns, they leave the church because they are devotees of his and not of the Saviour.

We have a biblical illustration of this truth in chapter 8 of the book of Acts. You will remember that in the city of Samaria, Simon the sorcerer was the great hero of the people. It was he who was able to perform tricks of magic. Because of this they literally genuflected at his feet. They felt that he was a god and worshiped him as such. Then Philip the deacon came to the city and began a mass evangelistic effort among the people. As a part of his crusade he cast out unclean spirits from those who were demon possessed; he caused the palsied to be healed and made the lame to walk. Naturally, the people were enamored with Philip, and they forgot all about Simon the sorcerer. They fell in love with this man that had done so many wonderful things in their midst.

In verse 12 of this chapter we read these words: *But when they believed Philip preaching the good news about the kingdom of God and the name of Jesus Christ, they were being baptized, men and women alike.* Notice the first part of that verse: *But when they believed Philip preaching the good news about the kingdom of God.* Philip is in the locative case. This case is exactly what you would surmise it to be. It is the case of location. Actually, what that verse is saying is this: "But when they put their faith in Philip as he preached the good news about the kingdom of God." These people did not put their faith in the Christ that Philip preached. Philip was the object of their belief. They transferred their allegiance from Simon the sorcerer to Philip the evangelist and deacon.

When Peter and John came from Jerusalem and began to investigate the situation, they discovered that these people had never been converted. Then they talked to them about the Holy Spirit—for they recognized what everyone needs to realize today, that no one can be converted without being both born and baptized by the Third Person of the Trinity. When they learned that the Samaritans knew nothing about Him, they personally led them to Christ, and as a result the Holy Spirit came upon them. The point that I want to make here is this: these people did what so many people do today; they put their faith in the preacher rather than in the Person, the Lord Jesus Christ, about whom the preacher was telling them. Their faith was falsely fixed in the pulpiteer and not the Saviour.

It was my privilege from 1950 to 1954 to be the pastor of the First Baptist Church in Pomona, California. This is a great church. My good friend Dr. Ted Cole has been pastor ever since I left there, and has done a marvelous job. Pomona First is one of the outstanding evangelical organizations in America.

While I was pastor of that church, I did a little research project. Meticulously I studied the history of the church. In so doing I discovered some very interesting things. For example, I found that when Dr. Gordon Palmer was the pastor there, many new people joined the church. A number of these, however, left just as soon as Dr. Palmer resigned. (This to my mind proved that they were not Christians.) This was not the fault of Dr. Palmer for he preached the unsearchable riches of the Lord Jesus Christ in a most uncompromising manner. He pled with people to put their eyes upon Christ and their faith in Him. However, because he was so magnetic in his presentation, there were many that did not see the Saviour that he was preaching. They only saw him. They became Palmerites and not Christians.

Then when Dr. Frank Kepner came he, too, was a great preacher. There were many people who were enamored with his preaching. They, therefore, made public decisions and were baptized into the membership of the church. However some of them never saw the Christ that Dr. Kepner preached; they only saw him. When he resigned as the pastor, the Kepnerites left with him proving that they had never had a born again experience. They were unconverted church members.

Hubert Davidson followed Frank Kepner. He was also an excellent pulpiteer. Under his ministry the church's evangelistic outreach was most effective. Great numbers became members. While most of these were truly converted, there were those who were simply drawn to Dr. Davidson and not to the Saviour whom he exalted. When he resigned, they became conspicuous by their absence. These people not only disassociated themselves from the local church there, but they did not associate themselves with any other. They simply dropped out of the picture as far as the Lord's work was concerned. They were Davidsonites not Christians.

One of the last messages I gave to the First Baptist Church in Pomona before I resigned was a sermon in which I reviewed this history. Telling them about the losses sustained because of the Palmerites, Kepnerites and the Davidsonites over the years, I pled with them to fall in love with Jesus Christ. I urged them to forget Harold Fickett except as a friend and a former pastor, but to make the Lord preeminent in their lives. I told them that the only hope they had for eternal life was through Him. I prayed, I trusted and I hoped that this message would get through to them. It did as far as the majority were concerned. However, when Dr. Cole came, there were those who left, simply because they were Fickettites and not Christians.

The sequence leading to membership follows the biblical pattern: conversion, baptism and then church membership.

Let me just point out that Dr. Palmer, Dr. Kepner, Dr. Davidson and I all had the same desire: we wanted the people to whom we ministered to fall in love with the King of kings and Lord of lords. Although I am sure that most of them did, there were some who remained unconverted because they had their eyes focused on us rather than upon the Christ whom we preached.

In the First Baptist Church in Van Nuys we are making an honest effort to prevent the developing of Fickettites. We are concerned that each individual who comes forward in our church makes his decision not for the pastor but for the Lord Jesus Christ. We realize that we are not 100% in achieving our goal of a regenerated church membership.

We do two important things, however, which greatly assist us at this point. In the first place, when a person publicly commits himself to Christ, we do not immediately vote him into our membership. Instead, he is taken into an interview room where a trained counselor deals with him concerning his experience of salvation. This interviewer stays with him until he is convinced that the person knows exactly what he is doing. Then he schedules a second interview for him. In this interview the counselor once again goes over the plan of salvation with him asking him if he has any questions about it, or any reservations concerning it. If there are questions the counselor does his best to answer them. If there are any reservations then the counselor, unless he can clear up these matters, will not recommend that he be admitted for church membership. Instead he will set up another interview with one of the pastors, so that he can help that person with his particular problem.

At the second interview the counselor also explains to the prospective new member the requirements of church membership. In this explanation he points out what his stewardship responsibilities are. He calls to his attention that he is to be faithful in attending the services; that he is to grow in grace and the knowledge of our Lord and Saviour Jesus Christ; and that he is to become involved in serving the Lord in one of the multiple facets of the church program. He also explains to him that we have a new members class which is not mandatory but which is available to him. This class runs for a period of seven weeks. A person can enter at any point during the cycle and then by attending seven weeks complete the course. We do not make this mandatory because we discovered that Baptists are not easily coerced.

I am reminded of the story of the Baptist preacher who was scheduled to preach in a Presbyterian church if he would wear a robe. And his response immediately was, "Do I have to?" When the answer came back negative he said, "Then I will be glad to wear it." We just don't coerce them into this new members class, but we try to lead them to take it, for we find that those who do are greatly helped in becoming the servants of Christ that God expects them to be.

In the second place, from time to time I emphasize from the pulpit that church membership does not save an individual. I point out that the person who is depending upon his membership for his salvation has only a false security. I call attention to the fact that both God and the individual know his true condition. In this connection I urge everyone to remember that God looks on the heart and not the outward appearance—that the individual can fool his fellow church members, but he cannot pull the proverbial wool over the eyes of the Almighty: *He* knows exactly what the situation is. In my invitation after preaching a message like this one, I plead with those who are unconverted church members to acknowledge Jesus Christ as their own personal Lord and Saviour. Many times after delivering a message of this type there are those who respond, who frankly tell me that their first decision was based on emotion and not on sincere born again experience.

About eleven years ago after I had finished preaching one Sunday night, I gave an invitation to all church members who were not converted to come forward and commit themselves to the Master. As the invitation began I noticed one of our deacons coming forward from the back of the sanctuary. If I had been asked at that time to make a list of the ten most pious, the ten most dedicated and the ten most used of the Lord deacons in our church—this man would have been near the top of the list. Perhaps I would have put him in first place. If I ever had a deacon in my church who really "deaced," this was the man. When he came to the front and I shook hands with him, I simply asked, "Are you coming to dedicate your life anew to Christ?"

He then astounded me; he replied, "No, pastor, I am coming to accept Christ as my Saviour and Lord. I know because of my multiple activities in the church you think I am a real Christian, that I have had a born again experience, but such is not the case. A few nights ago I began to examine my own life. I discovered that I am nothing but a hypocrite. I was living like a Christian. I was working like a Christian. I was serving God and the Church as a Christian should, but in my own heart I had never had a real conversion experience. That night I kneeled at the side of my bed, and I invited Jesus Christ into my heart as my Saviour and my Lord. I am coming tonight to make public confession of this and to ask the church to rebaptize me because the Bible teaches that conversion is to precede baptism." Naturally, we complied with his request.

I really learned a lesson out of this. I learned that only God and the individual really know what is on the inside. I am determined, therefore, that often in our services I am going to warn our people not to hide behind the false facade of church membership. I shall continue doing as I have so often done—plead with each of our members to make sure that he really knows Jesus Christ personally as his Saviour and Lord.

I know that we have a number of unconverted members in our church, even though I recognize that I am not to be the judge. I am aware that the Bible says, "Judge not, that ye be not judged." But I am also cognizant that the Scripture teaches us, "By their fruits ye shall know them." A pastor has to be a fruit inspector. After I inspect the fruit of some of those who claim to be Christians in our church, I am convinced that they have never had a born again experience. This weighs heavy upon my heart. I feel that they are my responsibility. Therefore, I must do all that I can to awaken them to their true condition, praying that they will allow the Holy Spirit to lead them into a right relationship with God.

Having said all of this, however, I do not want to leave the impression that church membership is not important; such is not the case, it is a "must" following conversion. Were this not true the apostle Paul wasted much of his time in his service to the Master. A careful review of his three missionary journeys reveals that he labored long and hard in establishing local churches in the communities which he visited. He was aware that the spread of the gospel in these localities after he had departed would be dependent upon these organizations. He not only loved the body of Christ, but he also had great affection for the organized churches that contributed to its growth and well being. Nine of the thirteen epistles he wrote are addressed to local churches.

It really grieves me—as a matter of fact it makes me just plain mad—to hear some super-pious person say, "I am part of the body of Christ; as far as I am concerned this is all that is important; church membership is of little consequence."

In one of my former pastorates a lady called me one day about three hours before a funeral that I was scheduled to conduct. In the course of our conversation she told me that she knew that members of the family of the deceased were not Christians. She suggested that a sound, evangelical, gospel message would be in order. After assuring her that I always emphasized God's plan of redemption in funeral sermons, I inquired, "And to what church do you belong?"

In a sickening, sweet voice she said, "Oh, I am a member of the body of Christ. I have looked all over this area for a church that suits me; but I just haven't found one. That is unimportant however. Just being a part of Christ's body is all that counts."

I had to remember that I was a gentleman, or I would have slammed down the receiver. Be assured that I terminated the conversation as quickly as possible. I then said to myself, "That woman is so heavenly she is no earthly good." I am sure the Lord Himself must have been nauseated at her pharisaical statements. Deliver me from people like this. If they do condescend to unite with the church, they are usually difficult to handle. At this point I am reminded of the preacher who said rather satirically, "I have only one spiritual member in my church, and she causes me more trouble than all the others put together."

The New Testament sequence is clear: conversion, baptism, church membership. The First Baptist Church in Van Nuys subscribes to this sequence and does its best to implement it.

CHAPTER 5

Confidence in the Leadership

In the fifth place much of the progress of our church is due to the fact that the people not only have confidence in the pastor and staff but also in the lay leadership. This enables us to operate not as a democracy but as a republic. Our form of government is the same as that of the United States. We have five boards which are elected by the church. These boards have been empowered to carry out the duties assigned to them without giving an account to the church except once a year in writing.

We elect a Deacons' Board. The members of this board are charged with the responsibilities of the communion services, manning the interview rooms, and of ministering to people who have made decisions for Christ and the Church. They also administer the social service funds. They call on the new members and assist in handling the various personal problems that arise within the membership.

We also elect a Trustee Board. The twelve men on this board are responsible for developing a budget and the handling of all funds that come into the church.

A School Board is elected which is charged with the responsibility of operating our Day School. (Parenthetically, let me say that this Board has nothing to do with the administration of our Sunday School. It is handled entirely by the professional staff that has been called to lead in the educational program of the church *per se.*)

We also have a Missions Board. Each year the trustees allocate so much money for Missions. They make known this allocation to the Missions Board which in turn develops a budget on the basis of it. In addition, our Missions Board sponsors our annual Missionary Conference. (Parenthetically, let me here point out that we have a Women's Missionary Fellowship whose president is elected by the church and therefore serves on the pastor's cabinet. This group through its board and circles works very closely with the Board of Missions in promoting all of our missionary causes. Mrs. Katie Coward, our Missions' administrator, is most adept at correlating the activities of the two groups. Through her skillful administration harmony prevails, and our missionary outreach is rapidly growing.)

We also have the Laymen's Council which is elected by the church. This council sponsors programs which are geared to promote fellowship within families and between family groups. For example, the council will have a night at a ball game for fathers and sons. And it will sponsor an evening in the gym for the fathers and daughters, or for mothers and sons. In addition, the council promotes and directs five golf tournaments a year and almost everything that has to do with the promotion of fellowship within our membership.

Each of these boards has a staff liaison that meets with it. Board night for all boards is the second Tuesday of each month. Just prior to these meetings, at 6:00 the board chairmen along with the other elected officers of the church meet for dinner with the administrator and myself as a Pastor's Cabinet. Following the meal each person gives a report of his board's activity, and on the basis of these reports we correlate the program. This enables us to eliminate scheduling conflicts or at least keep them to a minimum. Unfortunately, there are only seven days in the week.

There are three advantages to this republic form of church government rather than a democratic one. In the first place, this type of government enables us to eliminate the monthly business meetings that most evangelical churches conduct. Those who know anything about these business meetings are aware that they are probably the greatest block to progress that our churches face. For, usually when a business meeting is announced, if the people have an idea that it will be peaceful, only a few will come. One of my good Southern friends, a very prominent Baptist preacher, told me that when his church has a peaceful business meeting, only those who are ignorant of business principles attend. And even they are few in number. However, when a monthly business meeting is scheduled and the word is noised about that there is going to be a donnybrook, the sanctuary is crowded to the very back. The people choose up sides, and, "The fight is on, O Christian soldiers." Retrogression rather than progression inevitably results.

In the second place this form of government enables us to have a very short annual meeting. Usually we dispense with our business in about ten minutes. It consists of our administrator giving us a statistical review of what has taken place the year before, the election of church officers on the basis of nominations made by a committee and the acceptance of our budget. Printed reports from all the boards are made available immediately following the meeting. If they have any questions about these reports, they are instructed to call the office during the next week. It is rather interesting to me that during my twelve years here only one or two people have contacted our office with questions. And those have been of little consequence.

In the third place this type of government allows fast action to be taken when a situation arises that demands it. Let me give you four examples of what I mean by this:

First, from time to time in the course of a year we have had an emergency situation arise on the mission field where our missionaries have needed additional funds quickly. We have been able to provide these out of the contingency fund that is set up in the budget. Our Missions Board met, they approved the action, and the money was on its way. We did not have to wait until our monthly church business meeting in order to accomplish this.

The second example: five years ago it became apparent that we had to have a new Junior High building. The departments in this age group were growing so rapidly that we did not have facilities in which to house them. Our trustees considered the situation and found a way of providing the building. Even though we did not have money in our treasury, these dedicated business men, using the ingenuity that God had given them, devised a plan. They followed it, and the building became a fait accompli. As long as I live I shall never forget the thrill of standing in our pulpit on Wednesday night and announcing to our people that the trustees had decided to build a new Junior High building. I did not have to ask them for permission to do this. I simply told them that it was going to be done. And then I requested that they pray for the progress of the project. Not one single person objected to this. For, you see, the people in our church have confidence in the lay leadership.

The third example has to do with the Masonic building which is located just to the east of us and is bounded on the north and south by city streets. Through the years the Masons have been excellent neighbors. We have rented their parking lot on Sunday mornings and for brief periods of time have leased several of their rooms to be used for Sunday school purposes. We hold them in high esteem. Our rapport with them is excellent. I don't know of a church that has any better neighbors than they. Their property, however, is in our future plans. As a matter of fact, two years ago they painted their building the same color as ours. We immediately wrote and thanked them for this, assuring them that this would save us money in the future.

About seven or eight years ago I heard that the Masons were unhappy because they could not expand. As I considered the matter, I was willing for them to increase their facilities but not in that locality. I knew that if they were to do this the only way they could go was east. I therefore immediately called on the family that owned the acre and a quarter next to them. I told them that I was the pastor of the church on the corner, and we were interested in buying their property. I then asked them if they were willing to sell it and, if so, what would be the price. They replied that they had decided to sell because they wanted to move out of the San Fernando Valley. They had already talked about the price and had determined that it should be $87,000. I started bargaining with them. In so doing I was able to get them to reduce the selling price to $84,000.

I took it back to the trustees and explained the situation. One of the trustees asked the question, "Do you really think we need it?"

I said, "Oh, yes I am sure we do need it. Additional property is a must if we are going to grow."

He then asked, "Are you recommending that we buy it?"

My answer was negative, pointing out that we didn't have 84 cents to put down on it.

His reply made an indelible impression upon me; and it taught me an important lesson. Looking directly at me, he said, "Pastor, in our church if God needs something, we buy it. Then after we buy it we determine how we are going to pay for it. Once again I ask you as the pastor of this church, 'As you think about our future, do you really think we need the property?' "

And I responded in the affirmative. He then made the motion that the trustees buy it. Someone seconded the motion and it was unanimously carried.

Following this action I queried, "Now that we have bought it, how are we going to pay for it?" One of our trustees, a man in the escrow business who has great vision for our church, responded, "Let's ask the people for a long escrow. This will give us sufficient time to get the down payment." All agreed that this was a good idea.

The next day our church administrator, Mr. Ed Wilde, a very gifted man, contacted the people and told them that we wanted to buy the property and would do so if they would give us a long escrow. As he talked to them along this line, the wife said, "Isn't that interesting? We have purchased property in Oregon. We received a letter just today telling us that we could not occupy it for six months. My husband and I have agreed that if you will put $100.00 in escrow we will hold the property for you for this six months' period."

Church Boards and the Pastor's Cabinet make decisions regarding the administration, finances and discipline.

Literally, we scraped together the $100.00, placing it in escrow and securing the property for that length of time. At the end of the six months we had been able to accumulate enough to take care of the down payment and the property is now ours. But this is not the entire story.

About three months after we had purchased the property the city came through and rezoned that area. This meant that if we had waited three months more to buy the property we would have been looking at a price tag of somewhere between $225,000 and $250,000. Because the trustees were able to act quickly we saved that money. Had we had to argue this out in a monthly business meeting, I am convinced that we would still be discussing it—providing it had not been sold to some other buyer. Thank God for this type of government that enables us to act swiftly when the situation demands fast action.

The fourth example is related to church discipline. In the Gospel of Matthew, chapter 8, verses 15-17, our Lord Jesus Christ said, *And if your brother sins, go and reprove him in private; if he listens to you, you have won your brother. But if he does not listen to* you, *take one or two more with you, so that* BY THE MOUTH OF TWO OR THREE WITNESSES EVERY FACT MAY BE CONFIRMED. *And if he refuses to listen to them, tell it to the church; and if he refuses to listen even to the church, let him be to you as a Gentile and a tax-gatherer.*

The apostle Paul echoes these sentiments of Jesus as he writes in 1 Corinthians 5:1-5, *It is actually reported that there is immorality among you, and immorality of such a kind as does not exist even among the Gentiles, that someone has his father's wife. And you have become arrogant, and have not mourned instead, in order that the one who had done this deed might be removed*

56

from your midst. For I, on my part, though absent in body but present in spirit, have already judged him who has so committed this, as though I were present. In the name of our Lord Jesus, when you are assembled, and I with you in spirit, with the power of our Lord Jesus, I have decided to deliver such a one to Satan for the destruction of his flesh, that his spirit may be saved in the day of the Lord Jesus.

In these passages Jesus and the apostle Paul emphasize the necessity of church discipline. However, if you and I look at the contemporary ecclesiastical situation, we discover that most churches disregard these scriptural injunctions. Church discipline today is conspicuous by its absence. The reason for this is apparent. The leaders of churches recognize that when the entire church body administers discipline to one of its members inevitably this leads to a dichotomy which can easily eventuate into a split. The leadership of these churches would rather put up with flagrant violations of God's law than run the risk of tearing up their churches.

This is not true in the First Baptist Church in Van Nuys. Our Deacons' Board has been given the authority by the church to handle disciplinary matters. We have a permanent committee of the board who takes care of this responsibility. There are three men who are gifted in personnel work supervising this committee. When a problem arises, we do not allow it to fester and become inflamed. These three men move in on it immediately and do whatever is necessary in order to handle it. I have watched with avid interest their work.

They have been used of God in administering discipline in a manner which has brought glory to His name. They have handled such delicate problems as that of relieving Sunday school teachers of their duties, asking people to leave the choir and getting others to confess their immoral practices and seek forgiveness. Those they have disciplined have not been publicly embarrassed because their cases have been secretly handled. They have successfully rehabilitated a number whom they have disciplined to the point that they are now useful servants of the Lord in our church. We have avoided divisions because of their actions, and consequently have had no splits.

As a matter of fact, to my knowledge we have not even had any conversation about the committee's activities on the part of our general membership. By this method redemptive discipline is administered in our church in decency and in order. In a democracy this is an impossibility. In a republic it works. Thank God for the confidence our members have in the leadership of the church.

CHAPTER 6

Scripturally Financed

The financial structure of any church is of paramount importance to its success. I am convinced that one of the reasons that God is blessing the First Baptist Church in Van Nuys is because we are biblically financed.

We do not have any commercial schemes for raising money. For example, we do not put on dinners for that purpose. God is not in the restaurant business. Oh, yes, we serve meals. We are a typical Baptist Church. We are like the army. We move on our stomachs. But we do not attempt to make any profit through this means. We only try to break even. In the twelve years I have been here, however, we have been able to do this only on one or two occasions.

We do not have any rummage sales. God is not in the junk business. One of the cheapest things that a church can do is to try to pawn its junk out on the general public in order to enhance its treasury.

About twenty years ago a pastor in Ocean City, New Jersey, was having trouble with a very affluent woman, the president of his ladies' missionary society. She insisted on having rummage sales for her organization. One Sunday morning the pastor decided he was going to cure this once and for all. In his announcements he stated that they would have a rummage sale for the benefit of Mrs. So-And-So, the president of his missionary society. He went on to tell the people that they were to bring all of their junk to the church, that it would be sold to the general public and that the funds would be used to pay the personal and household bills of this woman. You can well imagine what happened after that service.

Like a chicken that had been roughed up, with her feathers high, she came charging down the aisle and accosted the pastor. Coldly staring into his eyes, she shouted, "Man, you know I don't need any money to pay my personal bills or my household bills. I have never been so embarrassed in all my life. How dare you announce a rummage sale to benefit me?"

The pastor very quietly replied, "Evidently you think you are superior to the Lord."

She asked, "What do you mean by that?"

He said, "You do not hesitate to put the pressure on me to have rummage sales to benefit His program. Surely, if it is good enough for the Lord Jesus Christ, it's good enough for you." This terminated the conversation. There was nothing left for her to say. She did an about-face and beat a hasty retreat. From then on, he had no more trouble with her.

Almost every working day in my office I receive, through the mail, propositions designed to get the membership of our church involved in some commercial scheme that promises to benefit us financially. I never take these to any of our boards. I have one file for them called the trash basket. We are just not interested in any man-made program for financing our activities.

In my opinion, there is only one way to underwrite the budget of the church and that is by the tithes and offerings of the people who love the Lord Jesus Christ and want to worship Him through giving. Ours is a tithing church. We believe that the person who refuses to give the Lord the tithe which is rightfully His is just as guilty of stealing from God as if he were to come to the communion table after the eleven o'clock service on Sunday morning and take money out of the offering plates that had been placed there.

In taking this position, we are simply echoing the teaching of Malachi as he wrote in chapter 3 of the book that bears his name, verses 8-10. There we read, *Will a man rob God? Yet you are robbing me! But you say, "How have we robbed Thee?" In tithes and contributions. You are cursed with a curse, for you are robbing Me, the whole nation of you. Bring the whole tithe into the storehouse, so that there may be food in My house, and test Me now in this, says the Lord of hosts, if I will not open for you the windows of heaven, and pour out for you a blessing until there is no more need.*

Several months ago we had Bob Harrington, the chaplain of Bourbon Street, in our church for an evangelistic crusade. In the course of one of his messages he told the story about being in the First Baptist Church in New Orleans, Louisiana. That particular evening he had preached on the subject of tithing. After the service, a deacon came to him and said, "Brother Bob, I want you to kneel with me, here at the altar, and pray with me about tithing."

Bob inquired of the deacon as to how long he had been serving on the board. When the man told him ten years, Bob quizzed him, "Do you mean you want me to kneel down here at the altar and close my eyes and pray with you about tithing?" When the man affirmed that he did, Bob continued, "I wouldn't do that for the world. For if I did, you would steal me blind, just as you have been stealing from God during this decade." Yes, the man that refuses to tithe is guilty of robbing God.

When I was pastor of the First Baptist Church in Coatesville, Pennsylvania, one Sunday morning I preached a sermon to this effect. The next day, a friend of mine, an executive of the big steel company in that city, came by my house to see me. He was greatly troubled over what I had said the day before. In the course of our conversation, he said to me, "Tell me, preacher, what do you mean by tithing? All of my life I have been in Sunday school and church, I have heard that term used by Sunday school teachers and preachers over and over, but I don't understand what it really means."

I replied, "Let me explain it to you by using myself as an example. My salary at the present time is about $700 a month. In addition, the church furnishes me a parsonage which is worth $200 a month. In other words, my compensation from the church is $900 per month. My tithe to the church on the basis of this salary is $90 per month. And in addition to the tithe, my wife and I delight to give an over and above offering."

With evident astonishment he said, "You mean you give ten per cent of your gross income?"

"That's right," I responded. "That's what tithing is, and unless you as a Christian are willing to do that you are guilty of robbing the Almighty." He went away shaking his head.

As we look about the Christian world today, we discover that the majority of those who claim to love the Lord Jesus are guilty of stealing from Him. It is said that if the average evangelical church had all of its members on welfare and each one tithed his welfare check, the budget of that average church would be three to five times more than it presently is.

My father is a very practical man. Several months ago he was serving as an interim pastor in a small Baptist church down in south Texas which was receiving between six and eight hundred dollars a Sunday in its offerings. Financial difficulties were arising because this was not sufficient to meet the needs. They brought this problem to Dad and asked him what he would suggest be done about it. He came up with the idea that they should have a tithing demonstration Sunday.

On that Sunday, as he envisioned it, he would do his best to get all of the people, whether they were tithers or not, to bring a tithe of their weekly income to the church for that one day. Feeling this was a good idea they announced the tithing demonstration Sunday. Great publicity was put out about it for several weeks prior to the day. Dad spoke of it from the pulpit. He urged everyone to give a tithe for that Sunday, whether this was their regular practice or not. On that particular day, they demonstrated their potential. Instead of the offering being $600.00 to $800.00, it was actually $3,395.00! These statistics proved conclusively that some—in fact quite a few people—in that church had been stealing from God.

As a pastor who believes in tithing, as a pastor who preaches tithing, I often have parsimonious church members come to me and say, "Preacher, don't you know that tithing is a matter of the law? We are living under grace. We are free. To tithe is to adhere to the law, therefore, count me out. Tithing is not for me."

Usually when someone makes such a statement I know immediately that he is merely using this as an excuse for not carrying his share of the financial load in the church. My response to this argument is, "Yes, tithing was incorporated into the law but tithing did not originate with the law. Tithing began long before the law came into being. For God had written into the hearts of righteous men the principle of tithing before He gave the commandments to Moses. For example, Abraham, long before Moses delivered the law to the people of Israel, gave his tithes to Melchizedek who is a type of the Lord Jesus Christ. Jacob tithed before the law came into being. Following this, tithing was made a part of the law and Malachi, the prophet, spoke about it."

As we turn to the New Testament, we discover that our Lord Jesus Christ was usually scathing in His denunciation of the scribes and the Pharisees in His day. However, there was one thing for which He applauded them and that was their tithing. In Matthew 23:23 we read where Jesus said, *Woe to you, scribes and Pharisees, hypocrites! For you tithe mint and dill and cummin, and have neglected the weightier provisions of the law: justice and mercy and faithfulness; but these are the things you should have done without neglecting the others.* Notice the statement *these are the things you should have done.* This was the one thing they did that pleased Jesus Christ. And I am here to tell you now that the Master is pleased when His own people honor Him with their tithes and with their offerings.

Back in 1961 my mother went to be with the Lord. One of the richest spiritual experiences that I have ever had occurred shortly thereafter. I had the privilege of going through her well-marked Bibles and studying the remarks she made in the margins. In one of them I made this previous discovery concerning tithing, "Abra-

ham commenced it, Jacob continued it, Moses confirmed it, Malachi commanded it, Jacob continued it,
Moses confirmed it, Malachi commanded it and Jesus
commended it."

Through the years I have been the pastor of the
First Baptist Church of Van Nuys it has been our poli-
cy during the month of either October or November to
have what we call "Operation Money." In that particular month I preach three sermons on the stewardship of
giving. In each of the services Sunday morning, Sunday
night and Wednesday night we give the people an opportunity to sign their commitment cards indicating the
amount of money that they feel God would have them
give during the coming year. It has been on the basis
of these commitments that our trustees have formulat-
ed the budget each year.

This past year, we did something different. We had
"Operation Money" during the month of November,
and I preached my usual three stewardship sermons.
However, when we passed out our commitment cards,
we did not ask the people to indicate the amount
which they were going to give during the coming year.
Instead we simply asked them to indicate that they
were willing to tithe that which God would provide for
them. In the event they were not willing to check this,
we had another place for them to check indicating that
they would give regularly to the church.

Interestingly enough, during this year when we are
facing in the San Fernando Valley an economic depres-
sion, with an 8.5 percent unemployment factor and
with many of our men without jobs, we are giving con-
siderably more than we have ever done before. I believe that this is due in part to the fact that Almighty
God has honored us for this new modus operandi. Because we did not ask them to indicate an amount but
to take a step of faith and commit themselves to tith-

ing, many people did so. It's the increased tithing that has increased our giving. As far as I am concerned, we will never go back to the old system of asking people to indicate specific amounts. Instead, our commitment cards will be based entirely on a tithing approach.

Leonard E. Hill, when illustrating the purchasing value of tithing, tells the following story: "John Rascus gave $100.00 when the offering plate was passed on a particular Sunday morning and in doing so he whispered, 'I'll see you in heaven.' Some seated nearby overheard. 'John Rascus is getting old,' they smiled to themselves. Later, when they told friends what John had said, all agreed, 'He'll find that money in a lot of places, but he'll never see it in heaven.'

"Oh, John Rascus went to heaven all right. No one had doubted that he would. There was no finer man in the church. It was a pity there were not more Christians like him. When the heart attack claimed him the next Sunday afternoon, everyone was sure John Rascus was united with his Master—but not with his money! You see, something happened to his offering.

"Seventy dollars never got out of Rascus's hometown. Some of it ended up in the Electric Service Company's bank account—the church used a lot of electricity. Bill Adams, the janitor, spent some of it after collecting his salary. A service station operator put a little of the money in his cash register after the preacher bought gas for his car.

"The thirty dollars which got outside Rascus's hometown went to some strange places. Some went to Nashville, Tennessee, to buy literature from the Sunday School Board for use by the church's members. A small amount went to a nearby college that Baptists owned. The treasurers at the Baptist Seminary didn't know it, but some of John Rascus's hundred dollars passed

The First Baptist Church of Van Nuys is financed by
families who follow the biblical principle of tithing.

through their hands when they paid seminary professors' salaries.

"Several dollars were soon in a bank being exchanged for some peculiar looking foreign currency. 'This is for overseas mission work,' someone said.

"It would be difficult to say exactly where all of John Rascus's offering went. Not that detailed records aren't available—it just scattered to so many different places. But one thing was certain as far as his fellow church members were concerned—it didn't get to heaven!

"At least that is what they thought. But John Rascus didn't agree. It took time, but he recovered his investment.

"The first returns came in dramatic fashion. One day a man warmly embraced John and shook his hand. 'Thank you! Thank you! Thank you!' he repeated.

"It seems this man had been a pretty lonely fellow down on earth. He didn't have much to do with anybody and nobody had much to do with him. That was before he saw the church light one Sunday night at John Rascus's church.

" 'I was awful lonely and tired of life,' he told John. 'I just went inside the church to get out of the dark for a while. But before I left, the darkness was gone out of me. During the service, I became a Christian.'

" 'Hmmmmm,' thought Rascus, 'I guess I got more out of the electricity than the Electric Service Company.'

"The next return on his investment was a surprise even to John. He had expected a return, but not exactly the way it happened. He was greeted by the young fellow who used to run the service station where John Rascus's pastor bought gas. He told John that he and the preacher talked a lot while the gas tank was filling. 'The preacher finally led me to Christ,' he said.

" 'More will come from that money,' mused Rascus. 'All those visits a car helped the preacher make will bring in more souls before long. I hadn't even thought of the service station fellow.'

"Soon it was a steady stream. Men, women, boys, girls—won to the Lord by young ministers just out of the seminary; Sunday school teachers grateful for the help good literature gave them in teaching the Bible; people of strange dress and features who had learned of Christ from missionaries. All had a 'thank you' for John.

"John Rascus is still collecting his money.

"Yet there are some people who think John wasted a lot of money by putting it in the offering plate—especially when all it went for was to pay electric bills, salaries and other such ordinary things."

An anonymous writer has stated that "the tither has six surprises in store for him. First, at the deepening of his spiritual life in paying the tithe. Second, at the ease in meeting his obligations with nine tenths of his income. Third, at the amount of money he has for the Lord's work. Fourth, at the ease in going from one tenth to larger giving. Fifth, at the preparation that tithing gives to be a faithful and wise steward over the nine tenths that remain, and sixth, at himself, in that he had not adopted the plan sooner."

Several years ago I read this story of a southern rural church. The man who owned the mill which ginned the cotton for all of the farmers of that area was asked to be the treasurer of the church. He said that he would do so if he were allowed to operate its finances for an entire year without giving any report as to what he was doing until the year had been completed. The members of the church had great confidence in this man and they readily agreed to this proposition.

During the year of his administration of the funds, tremendous things happened in that church. They were able to build a new educational unit. They refurbished the parsonage. They doubled their missionary giving, and they redecorated their sanctuary. All of the members were greatly pleased by these achievements.

At the annual business meeting at the end of that year, they called upon the treasurer to give his report and in so doing, to explain how he had been able to accomplish so much with what they had given.

Quietly, the man began to speak. "All of you have been tithing this year, even though you do not know it. As you farmers have brought your cotton to my gin, I have set aside 10 percent of it for the Lord. I have ginned the 90 percent for you and given you the proceeds from it. The 10 percent I ginned for the Lord I sold and used the proceeds in His service. Through tithing, our church has been able to accomplish far more this year than any other previous year in our history. And the interesting thing to me is this. None of us has missed the 10 percent. You have tithed without knowing it. God has enabled you to use the nine tenths effectively, and the program of Jesus Christ has gone forward."

I can personally testify to the fact that God not only blesses the church that tithes but He also pours out His blessings upon the individual who is obedient to Him in this regard.

When my wife and I were first married, I was a Senior at the Southern Baptist Theological Seminary in Louisville, Kentucky. During this year, I was serving two pastorates in southern Indiana. My total compensation for this work was $65 a month. I had to drive 200 miles each weekend to collect this. In addition to driving the 200 miles I also had to pay fifty cents each way to cross the Ohio River. My father, during the last year of my seminary life, gave my wife and me $25 per month to pay our rent. (Prices were low in those days.) In other words, my total compensation was $90 per month. My wife and I began immediately to give the Lord the first one tenth—nine dollars each month for His work. As I look back on this, I am thrilled that I was obedient to the Lord's financial directive. Day by day, since that time, He has given me an increasingly exciting, exhilarating and satisfying ministry. As time marches on, it gets better and better.

You will notice that in this testimony I pointed out that my wife and I gave the first one tenth of our income to the Lord. Oftentimes I have had church members say to me, "Pastor, I believe in tithing. I know God has directed me to do so. I am convinced that when I fail to tithe I am disobedient to Him and therefore outside of His will. Having said all of this, however, I must point out that after I pay my rent, my grocery bill, my doctor, my dentist, my gasoline bill, my car payment and all the other daily incidentals that are incumbent upon me, I don't have one tenth left to give to the Lord. I can assure you that if I had 10 percent of my income over and above what my expenses are, I would surely give it to Him."

I always point out to such people that they have the cart before the horse. Nobody in average circumstances, if he pays all of his expenses before he gives to the Lord that which is rightfully His, will ever fulfill his tithing responsibility. In order for us to be pleasing to the Lord, it is necessary to give the first one tenth to Him. This is the burden of my preaching. I urge the people of the First Baptist Church to do this, and many of them do. This enables us to continually expand our program.

One of the saddest sights in Christendom today is that of a man who at one time in his life served the

Lord with his time, his talents and his tithe, but now his heart has grown cold. He is not involved in doing anything for the Saviour. Unfortunately, legion is the number of people like this.

Dr. C. Roy Angel, in his book *Apples of Gold and Pitchers of Silver*, repeats a story that Dr. W. D. Nolan, one of the veteran preachers in Florida, told him.

Said Dr. Nolan, "John, a fine young man in our church, was the superintendent of our Sunday school. He had the esteem and the confidence of the whole town. When he opened his own business, he prospered immediately. He was an outstanding Christian who never missed a service. He was active in all the departments of the church. He was a consistent tither and one of the most faithful stewards in our entire organization. His business had succeeded so that he moved into larger quarters. At the end of the second year he opened a branch store in the next town. In the meantime his tithe grew until he was by far our largest giver. At the end of four years he had opened six branch stores and his tithe had grown to $100.00 a week, but there his contribution stopped.

"At that point he asked to be released from the superintendency of the Sunday school until he could get his business organized better. He also stopped coming to the prayer meetings and then we began to miss him at church on Sunday.

"When I went to see him he told me that his business demanded so much of his time that often he spent the weekends in one of the other towns getting things organized. Though his income grew larger, his contribution stayed at $100.00 a week.

"One day I went down to his office. I closed the door behind me as I went in. I said to him, 'John, I am worried about you. You are missing church and apparently you are losing interest in the Kingdom's work, and I am afraid that you are not giving your tithe to the Lord any longer.'

"He replied, 'Brother Nolan, my tithe is too big, and I thought $100.00 a week was enough to give to the Lord's work. My business is so large that I don't have as much time as I used to have.'

"I answered, 'John, will you get down here on your knees and pray with me?' After we knelt, I began the prayer like this, 'Dear Lord, you have prospered John too much. You have given him too much business and too much success. His tithe is too big to give to you. So dear Lord, for John's sake and for the Kingdom's work, burn down some of his stores. Let some of them fail. Take away some of the business from him so he can be the same John we used to love and who used to work so faithfully for you.'

"I felt John tremble a little and then he spoke out, 'Mr. Nolan, let me take it up from here.'

"His prayer was one that came from a contrite and very humble heart. He asked God's forgiveness. He promised he would do it differently from now on.

"John came back to his place as the superintendent of the Sunday school. Once again he became a regular attender of all the services, and he began to give the Lord the full tithe which was rightfully His."

As I read that story, a prayer formed within my heart. "Oh, God, give us many, many more like this young man John."

As far as I am concerned, my position as pastor of the First Baptist Church in Van Nuys on the subject of tithing is exactly the same as that taken by Dr. Fred E. Brown many years ago. In expressing his position, Dr. Brown wrote, "I make no apology for lifting the scriptural standard of giving to Christian people, for I seek not yours but you. In my experience as pastor, I have never known a Christian who has read his Bible regularly, prayed daily, attended church faithfully and tithed his income who was unhappy."

"The tithe is the Lord's." You say you don't see it that way? Possibly not, but the Bible says, "The tithe is the Lord's." You say that you are in debt? Yes, but the Bible says, "The tithe is the Lord's." You say, but I have dependents and other obligations that nobody knows about? That may be true. Heroically, unselfishly, sacrificially, you may be caring for others. But the Bible says, "The tithe is the Lord's." Whatever one may say or think, the Bible answers back, "The tithe is the Lord's."

How much should you subscribe? I don't know. But I do know the portion of your income which the Bible says belongs to God, "The tithe is the Lord's." If every evangelical Christian would subscribe to this and act upon it, the ministry of evangelical Christianity would be greatly enhanced. We would be able to send far more missionaries to the foreign fields than we are presently sending. Our outreach for Christ throughout the world would become more effective, and our local church programs would begin to get the job done that God intends for us to do.

I close this chapter much as I began it. One of the main reasons that God has blessed the First Baptist Church in Van Nuys is because this is a tithing church. In making this statement I do not claim that every member of our church is a tither. But we are working on it, and we will not be content until this is a reality.

CHAPTER 7

Adequately Staffed

The membership in the First Baptist Church in Van Nuys subscribes to the idea that the pastor must have an adequate staff in order to get the job done that God has called him to do. No church, regardless of how small it may be, can be handled by one individual. Or to put this another way, no man is capable by himself of handling even the smallest church. He needs a staff either on a voluntary or a paid basis.

As we look into the Old and New Testaments we discover biblical precedent for staffing a church so that its program can run smoothly and effectively. For example, in chapter 11 of the book of Numbers we have the story of the children of Israel wandering in the wilderness complaining against Moses because they did not like the bill of fare provided for them by the Almighty.

We read in verses 4-9, *And the rabble who were among them had greedy desires; and also the sons of Israel wept again and said, "Who will give us meat to eat? We remember the fish which we used to eat free in Egypt, the cucumbers and the melons and the leeks and the onions and the garlic, but now our appetite is gone. There is nothing at all to look at except this manna." Now the manna was like coriander seed, and its appearance like that of bdellium. The people would go about and gather it and grind it between two millstones or beat it in the mortar, and boil it in the pot and make cakes with it; and its taste was as the taste of cakes baked with oil. And when the dew fell on the camp at night, the manna would fall with it.*

These people did everything to the manna they could possibly do in order to have a diversified diet. However, they were not satisfied with it. They wanted some meat to eat. And they didn't have it. The result of their griping is described for us in verses 10-15 of that same chapter:

Now Moses heard the people weeping throughout their families, each man at the doorway of his tent; and the anger of the Lord was kindled greatly, and Moses was displeased. So Moses said to the Lord, "Why hast Thou been so hard on Thy servant. And why have I not found favor in Thy sight, that Thou hast laid the burden of all this people on me? Was it I who conceived all this people? Was it I who brought them forth, that Thou shouldest say to me 'Carry them in your bosom as a nurse carries a nursing infant, to the land which Thou didst swear to their fathers'? Where am I to get meat to give to all this people? For they weep before me, saying 'Give us meat that we may eat!' I alone am not able to carry all this people, because it is too burdensome for me. So if Thou art going to deal thus with me, please kill me at once, if I have

80

*found favor in Thy sight, and do not let me see my
wretchedness.*"

The burden of caring for the children of Israel
weighed so heavily upon Moses that he told the Almighty he would rather die than carry it any longer.
This is often the case of a pastor with his church. Bur-
dens that are placed upon him by the membership become so intolerable, so heavy, that he would rather do
almost anything than remain at the helm of the church.

The way God handled this problem, as far as Moses
was concerned, is recorded in Numbers 11:16-25. God
had a rather ingenious plan. He told Moses that He
recognized that carrying the burden of the entire nation was too much for him—that he needed assistance.
He therefore suggested that seventy men of the elders
of Israel who were respected by the people be selected
by Moses. God said *I will take of the Spirit who is
upon you, and will put* Him *upon them; and they shall
bear the burden of the people with you, so that you
shall not bear it all alone.*

The great emancipator was delighted. We read that,
*So Moses went out and told the people the words of
the Lord. Also, he gathered seventy men of the elders
of the people, and stationed them around the tent.
Then the Lord came down in the cloud and spoke to
him; and He took of the Spirit who was upon him and
placed* Him *upon the seventy elders. And it came
about that when the Spirit rested upon them, they
prophesied. But they did not do it again.* God solved
Moses' problem by having staff members assigned to
him who could assist him in meeting the demands incumbent upon him as the leader of Israel.

We find a similar situation in chapter 6 of the book
of Acts. You may remember that the members of the
Ladies' Missionary Society of the church in Jerusalem
were embroiled in a conflict. The Grecian widows were

complaining that the Hebrew widows were receiving preferential treatment in the dispensing of the social service funds. They wanted this situation rectified. They demanded that it be done immediately.

Naturally, the problem was presented to the apostles who were giving leadership to the church. The response on the part of these men was a classic. It is recorded for us in verses 2-4: *And the Twelve summoned the congregation of the disciples and said, "It is not desirable for us to neglect the word of God in order to serve tables. But select from among you, brethren, seven men of good reputation, full of the Spirit and of wisdom, whom we may put in charge of this task. But we will devote ourselves to prayer, and to the ministry of the word."*

In effect, the apostles said that they knew that this problem needed to be handled, but that they were too busy with the task assigned them by Almighty God to deal with the situation. They needed a staff to assist them. They, therefore, suggested that seven men from the congregation be appointed as their assistants.

They laid down three requirements for these men. First, they were to be men of honest report—men whose word was as good as their bond. Second, they were to be men who were filled with the Holy Spirit. And third, they were to be filled with wisdom. Someone has suggested that this third requirement might be translated, "They were to be filled with sanctified common sense."

This suggestion pleased the people, and they selected a staff of seven—Stephen, Philip, Prochorus, Nicanor, Timon, Parmenas and Nicolas, a proselyte from Antioch.

Immediately these seven staff members began working on the problem. They were eminently successful, and the results were tremendous. They are described for us in verse 7, *And the word of God kept on spreading; and the number of the disciples continued to increase greatly in Jerusalem, and a great many of the priests were becoming obedient to the faith.*

By having an adequate staff, the apostles were able to continue their ministry of prayer, and the teaching and preaching of the Word of God. At the same time the problems within the church were handled in a proper manner.

When my wife and I moved to Boston and were looking for a new home, the real estate man who took us in tow said one day, "There are three requirements for a good home. The first is location, the second is location, and the third is location." Let me paraphrase this for you. There are three requirements for a good program within the church. The first is leadership, the second is leadership and the third is leadership. If the church has the proper staff that can give guidance to the various facets of the program, inevitably that church is going to grow.

Members of the First Baptist Church in Van Nuys recognize this. And they have given me not only an adequate staff but a superb one. As a matter of fact, they subscribe to the basic conviction, which is also mine, that the larger the church grows, the more staff members the church needs.

We operate on the basis that when a program is to be started, the first thing that must be done is to select the proper leadership for it. Without this, it cannot get off the ground. We have discovered that every time we have put on a new staff member to man a program, additional members have been brought into the church through his efforts. And as the result, we have had no difficulty in paying his salary. In fact, our trustees who are in charge of the finances will not initiate any new outreach until the proper leadership is selected for it.

This type of modus operandi has been paying dividends in our church—it is paying dividends—and, I am confident that it will continue to pay dividends in our church.

Let me document this for you. Just a little more than a year ago I was convinced that the Spirit of God wanted us to open a coffeehouse on Van Nuys Boulevard. This section of our city is almost as infamous as the Sunset Strip because of the prevalence of the sale and purchase of narcotics, nude bars, illicit sex and crime in general. Young people by the hundreds loiter along this boulevard every night. Most of these are not interested in attending church. They are simply out for what they call a "groovy" time. And yet God loves them and they need to be reached for Jesus Christ. As I thought and prayed about this I became convinced that our approach should be through a coffeehouse ministry. I shared this with our trustees. They agreed that we should go into this program, and they suggested that I begin to look for the proper staff member. But, as you might suspect, people that have had experience in this are rather hard to come by for it is a ministry that has developed only in recent years.

However, several months later, as I was visiting in the home of our college director, I was privileged to meet the father and mother of his lovely wife. In talking to them I was greatly impressed by their understanding of the Scripture, their deep consecration, and their magnetic personalities. My wife and I were quickly drawn to them by their charismatic Christian spirits.

In the course of the conversation I asked them what they had been doing. The man responded, "We have been conducting a coffeehouse ministry in Heidelberg, Germany, under the auspices of the Youth for Christ program. Our ministry has been to the American servicemen who are stationed in that area." When they told

When the coffeehouse ministry was begun, God provided an experienced man to direct the activities.

me this, lights went on in my head and bells began to ring. I was so excited I could hardly contain myself. I didn't mention what I had in mind, but I inquired, "What are you going to do now? Are you planning to take a pastorate or will you go to another mission field; or just what are your plans?" He replied that they were waiting for the direction of the Holy Spirit. Their only desire was to do God's will.

I went to our trustees at the next meeting and told them about this couple. I suggested that we could find no better people to lead our coffeehouse ministry than Reverend and Mrs. Cal Harrah. Without any hesitation they authorized me to employ him to direct this program. Although we didn't have any money for his salary, we stepped out on faith believing that when the coffeehouse ministry became a reality, God would provide the funds.

I immediately went to Reverend Harrah and shared with him the fact that we would like to call him to this ministry. I said, "It will be up to you to find the coffeehouse—it will be your responsibility to make all arrangements for it. It will be incumbent upon you to handle all the many details in connection with it, and to set up the program that it will follow."

It took him about four to five months to find the proper location, but he finally found it. All during this time we were paying him a salary. We were working with him and praying for him that the Holy Spirit would lead him to the place where this coffeehouse ministry should be conducted. I am convinced that God had him by the hand in this, for the location we now have is just right for such a ministry. We are just two doors south of the Happening, which is a nude bar, and eight doors south of the Bottoms Up, another nude bar. As Bob Harrington says about his ministry on Bourbon Street in New Orleans, "We don't have to take a census in that area to find where our prospects are."

After we leased the building, Reverend Harrah planned all the details as to how it was to be arranged. He has scheduled the nightly programs and has given direction to every facet of this outreach. And God has really blessed.

On Monday night before New Year's 1971, some of our kids in the coffeehouse, which has been named "the Mustard Seed" decided that they wanted to close down one of the nude bars just north of us. About forty of them went out on the street, knelt down in front of the bar and began to pray aloud. It wasn't long until two motorcycle policemen came and began to observe their activity. Neither one of them said anything. I don't blame them; there were only two officers and forty teenagers. They didn't know who these young people were and had no idea of their intentions.

Several minutes later two squad cars came up with two policemen in each of them. When finally the officers totaled six, they had the courage to speak out. One of them shouted at our kids, "What in the hell are you doing?" A young man from our group turned to the officer and said, "We are praying that God will close this dump down and that we will win the proprietor to Jesus Christ." The officer was flabbergasted. With a smile on his face and waving his hand he said, "More power to you." And all six of them drove off.

This really encouraged our kids. They turned on the volume and began to pray at the top of their voices. It wasn't long before a crowd had gathered around them. The patrons of the night club, hearing the commotion on the outside, ran out to see what it was all about. Finally a large group had surrounded our kids, and the kids got up off their knees and began to witness to them. Within a few moments five of them had prayed to receive Jesus Christ into their lives.

The owner of the night club came out and asked two of our fellows to go in with him to talk to him about the situation. One of our boys, in telling me about it, said, "It was rather strange. We and the proprietor were dressed but the girls in there who were standing around listening to what was being said were all naked. The proprietor opened the conversation. He was livid with anger. He shouted, 'What are you trying to do—close me down?' Tom (our boy) responded, 'No sir. We love you! We want to keep you out of hell! We are here to tell you about Jesus.' "

For fifteen minutes our fellows stayed in there and talked to the proprietor and the girls about the Saviour and His ability to transform their lives. When it became apparent that the proprietor was not going to buy the product that our fellows were seeking to give him, they beat a strategic retreat, leaving him standing there, talking to himself.

But this is not the whole story. New Year's Eve our guys and gals decided that they would have a March for Jesus down Van Nuys Blvd. When the owners of several of the bars heard about this they were apprehensive. They feared that our group might come into their places of business and witness to their patrons. They knew that they could not call the cops to protect them from the Christians. (That's a switch, isn't it? They were really afraid of these courageous kids!) Therefore on New Year's Eve, which should have been the most lucrative night in the entire year, both of these nude bars closed down. After the march, when our young people came to our midnight communion service at the church they were just thrilled because of what God had done through them.

This could never have happened had we not had an

adequate staff to begin this coffeehouse ministry and to implement its program. I don't have time to carry on a program like this. None of our other staff members have the time which they can devote to it. It takes one man to do this job. Since that time we have had to add Rick as a part-time assistant because the Lord continues to bless the program.

And let me tell you about Rick. At midnight he and one of his buddies were down on a parking lot in front of a big shopping center south of the Mustard Seed. They noticed that a gang of boys were taking turns kicking a pregnant girl in the stomach. As they watched, the Hell's Angels came up and began to fight off that gang. One of the Hell's Angels stepped in between the boy that was doing the kicking and the girl. When he did, the one who was kicking stabbed that Hell's Angel in the shoulder, in the side and in the thigh. After doing this he and the other members of his gang ran away. The Hell's Angels took their wounded buddy into the laundromat in that shopping center and they sewed him up with a regular needle and thread. Rick and a friend were there and took it all in. After the Hell's Angels had completed this crude suture job, Rick asked them, "What are you going to do with him?"

They said, "We don't have any idea." He then asked, "Don't you think you had better take him to the hospital?"

They said, "Oh no, if we did that, we would all be in trouble. We don't dare get involved with the establishment." And then they inquired, "Do you have any ideas what we can do with him?"

"Yes," Rick replied, "let us have him. We will take him down to the Mustard Seed and make a place on the floor for him to sleep tonight. We'll watch over him and if he is not better in the morning, we'll take him to the emergency ward in the Valley Hospital."

The Hell's Angels agreed to this. Actually, they were so glad that Rick was willing to do this that they gave him a Hell's Angel courtesy card. They told him that if he was ever in trouble and needed assistance just to call upon them, show that courtesy card and he would get all the help he required. Rick and his friend took this wounded Hell's Angel to the coffeehouse, followed by a girl that he had picked up that night—a street walker whom he called his wife. She was a pitiful character of about seventeen or eighteen years of age. She had run away from home. Her only way of making a living was to be a wife to any of the gang members who wanted her. They would provide for her if she accommodated them.

So that night, these two young men took that wounded Hell's Angel to the coffeehouse and made him as comfortable as possible and the girl was with them. They talked to both about Jesus. They witnessed to them and pled with them to accept Christ as their Saviour. Rick, in telling me about it, said that this injured boy would go to sleep, and they would quit talking. Then he would wake up, and they would start witnessing to him again. In the morning, because the boy was no better, they took him to the emergency ward in the Valley Hospital. The girl left, and they thought they would never see her again; but they were wrong.

Two months later, she came back to the Mustard Seed and gave this testimony. She said, "That night I listened to the boys in the coffeehouse tell about Jesus Christ and what he could do for an individual who would give his or her life to Him. They really impressed me with the message. I also took a copy of *Good News for Modern Man* with me when I left. I made my way back to Ohio. I was riding with two boys in a car going at a speed of ninety miles an hour over icy roads. I was in the back seat, reading the New Testament, and as I read it, the Lord Jesus Christ revealed Himself to me and I gave up my old way of life as I invited the Saviour into my heart. I began to pray that God would keep us in safety. I knew it wouldn't do any good to talk to the boys about slowing down. I was aware we were in danger because of the slickness of the road and the speed with which we were traveling. We skidded, but we didn't turn over, and I continued to pray. The we began to skid again and finally we came to an abrupt halt as we hit a snowbank; no one was hurt. I told those boys that the reason for this was because I had become a Christian in the back seat from thinking about the testimony I'd heard in the Mustard Seed and from reading the New Testament. I shared with them the fact that I had been praying for God's safe keeping. I told them that they too needed to accept Jesus Christ as their Saviour and Lord. They laughed at me. Nevertheless I stayed by my testimony.

"I went to my home in Ohio where I have a sister and her husband who are Christians. I shared with them what had happened to me. They helped me in my Christian life. I have now come back to California. I haven't come back here to get hooked on dope again and to live a life of prostitution. I haven't come back here to be a wife to any of the gang members who want me. I've come back here to work and live for Jesus Christ. I would like to volunteer to do anything in the Mustard Seed that will help you and will be of benefit to my Saviour."

This extension of the coffeehouse ministry to the parking lot in front of the shopping center would have been an impossibility had it not been for the willingness on the part of our church to put on another staff member to assist in the Mustard Seed's outreach. Rev.

Harrah would not have time to do that. He spends hours and hours seeing to it that the program in the Mustard Seed is what God would have it to be.

Just recently the Galpin Ford Company in our area gave us a panel truck for the Mustard Seed outreach. We have painted it psychedelically. We are going to use it as a mobile coffeehouse—going up and down the boulevard—parking it in various places, seeking to reach those who are loitering on the street with the gospel of the Lord Jesus Christ. It has been suggested that we call this "the Tumbleweed" out of "the Mustard Seed." That has not been determined, but we do know that the outreach of the Mustard Seed is going to be greatly enhanced as the result of this mobile facility.

Oftentimes I am asked by other churches to meet with their boards to discuss their programs. In speaking to the lay leaders of these churches, I find that all of them are in agreement that proper leadership is necessary for the success of any program. They are all well aware of the fact that a pastor cannot do the job by himself—that an adequate staff is necessary. Many times, however, I find that these same laymen have one hangup. It's the dollar mark. Even if they are convinced that the church needs a staff, because they cannot see the source of the money with which to employ the necessary personnel, they refuse to go ahead. In taking this position, they are really getting the cart before the horse. They don't seem to understand the fact that the way churches pay their bills is by increasing their membership. These new members then give more money with which to meet the financial obligations of the church. Any staff member who is worth his salt is able to produce his salary over and over again by the number of new members he brings into the church. I am convinced that the growth of many churches has been stunted because the laymen have prevented the pastor from employing the necessary personnel to staff the programs that should be started. I am thankful to God that the First Baptist Church in Van Nuys is not in this category. Our lay leaders are most helpful at this point. They have almost given me carte blanche as far as the securing of the staff is concerned. And it has really paid off for us. We now have 114 full and part-time workers as our colleagues in this ministry.

CHAPTER 8

Motivated by Faith

Oftentimes in a given community, two churches can be found that are similar in theology. They both preach the gospel. They both believe the Bible to be the Word of God. They both are concerned about winning people to a saving knowledge of Jesus Christ. They both manifest an interest in reaching young people for the Saviour, and they both have an insatiable desire to grow. Yet, one of these churches makes rapid advance, while the other does well to maintain the status quo. The question arises in such a situation: "Why is this?" And the answer can be summarized with one word. It is the word "faith."

In chapter 12 of 1 Corinthians, the apostle Paul, inspired by the Holy Spirit, gives us a list of the gifts of the Spirit. A careful perusal of this list reveals that the third gift is that of faith—faith, not in the sense of saving faith, but faith in the sense that William Carey used the term. Remember, he advised his colleagues to undertake great things for God and expect great things from God. This third gift of faith is that which motivates individuals and churches to undertake great projects for the Saviour, while at the same time, expecting tremendous blessing from Him. I am convinced that the Holy Spirit gives to each church this third gift of faith. To the extent that the church uses the gift and acts upon it, to that extent it grows and prospers in serving the Master.

In this connection it is rather interesting to note that the first person to question the validity of the virgin birth of Christ was not some professor who was educated beyond his intelligence. It was not some scientist who had difficulty in accepting the fact of miracles. Instead, it was Mary herself. She was lacking in faith at this point.

When the angel announced to her that she was to be the mother of the Christ child, she immediately began to question him. "But," she said, "this is an impossibility. I'm not married. I cannot have a child." As we look at the Gospel of Luke, chapter 1, verses 35-37, we hear the angel responding to Mary by saying, *The Holy Spirit will come upon you, and the power of the Most High will overshadow you; and for that reason the holy offspring shall be called the Son of God. And behold, even your relative Elizabeth has also conceived a son in her old age; and she who was called barren is now in her sixth month. For nothing will be impossible with God.*

Here we find the angel emphasizing the fact that if a person has faith to believe that God can do all things, miracles can occur. After the angel revealed this truth to Mary, she accepted it; and in Luke 1:38, Mary's response is recorded, *Behold, the bondslave of the Lord; be it done to me according to your word.* The virgin birth became a reality. Mary accepted God's ability at this point by faith, and she became the mother of the Christ child.

Any church which has faith to believe, like Mary, that with God all things are possible and is willing to act upon that faith, can accomplish that which appears to be impossible. The First Baptist Church in Van Nuys is such a church. As one reads through the history of the church, he sees multiple illustrations of this truth. Let me just share two with you by way of documentation.

Back in 1962, our preaching services were conducted in what we now call Barrington Hall. Actually it is our gymnasium. We were able to crowd only about 1,150 or 1,200 people into that space. Sunday morning after Sunday morning at our 11 o'clock services, we were turning people away. We just could not accommodate them. We found the same thing to be true many Sunday evenings. Naturally, as pastor, I was concerned about it, for I recognized that a church cannot maintain the status quo. It either progresses or it retrogresses. I was apprehensive lest people get discouraged because they could not be seated in the sanctuary and decide to go elsewhere.

In desperation, we tried closed circuit television into our chapel. I remember one day a little boy came up to me enthusiastically and said, "Pastor, do you mind if I go into the chapel and watch that short circuit television?" That boy was saying more than he knew, for as far as effectiveness was concerned that closed circuit television was a short-circuited proposition. The picture was dark. The people didn't feel a part of the service. It just didn't get the job done. At first when we started to use it, the chapel was filled. But it wasn't long until only a few were attending.

In desperation, I said to our trustees, "We must do something to provide a new sanctuary for ourselves. At that time, we had an indebtedness of $500,000.00, and we needed a sanctuary to accommodate at least 2,000. We employed a loan finder in Beverly Hills to look for loans for us, not only in the United States, but also in Canada. At one time, he came back from the offices of the Sun Life Insurance executives, saying that he had secured a loan. We were enthusiastic. However, when we got down to the nitty-gritty of dealing with these people about our situation, they were apprehensive. They felt that we already had more indebtedness than we could handle, so they decided not to go along with us. Our loan finder went to the John Hancock Insurance Company in Boston. He presented our case, only to be turned down.

Then he went to the American Life Insurance Company down in Galveston, Texas, the city where I was reared. When he put the stationery of our church on the desk of the secretary, and she took it in to the executive, my name was on it. That executive did not see the "Jr." He thought it was my father who was applying for the loan. Dad had a great reputation in Galveston. The First Baptist Church in that city always paid its bills on time. It had a credit rating that was superior. Thinking that the church that was applying for the loan was pastored by my father, the executive allowed our loan finder to come in and discuss our situation with him. After he heard the story, he simply said to our representative, "The best we can do for you is to offer you $500,000.00." When he came back and reported this, naturally we had to turn it down for it wasn't sufficient to meet our needs.

The situation grew increasingly worse as far as our ability to meet the needs of the people who wanted to attend our church was concerned. We tried three services. However we discovered that people are creatures of habit; that if they want to go to the 9:30 or the 11 o'clock service, they will go at that time. We could have as many other services as we desired, but they would not be present. We found that the early service did not give us any relief at all. I became more and more concerned about the situation because we were continually turning people away from our door.

Finally, one Tuesday morning when our staff was meeting for prayer, I said to my fellow workers, "This morning, let us pray simply for the loan; that God will enable us to find a place where money will be provided for us. Let's forget all other requests, and let us lay this one specifically before the Lord." I confess to you that I've never been in a prayer meeting where I felt a greater sincerity in prayer on the part of the people who were participating than in this one.

Immediately following this prayer service, my church administrator and I had a meeting with Mr. Bob Fuller, who was the president of the San Fernando Valley Federal Savings and Loan Company. This particular organization is located only about four blocks from our church. After we conducted our business with Mr. Fuller, I simply said to him, "Bob, why don't you take our full load?" Quizzically he asked, "And what is your full load?" I explained to him that we had a debt of $500,000.00, and that we needed a new sanctuary, which I contemplated would cost $1,100,000.00. I said, "Our full load, Bob, is to give us a loan of $1,600,000.00."

This man was a man of faith. He believed that churches added a great deal to the well-being of the community. He said to me, "I'm very much interested in picking up your full load. I'm sure that we can do it. We will have to get another fiduciary institution to join with us in making this amount available to you. But

I'm convinced that we will be able to find that other institution. You go on out from here and ask your architect to begin drawing the plans."

After I had pulled myself off the ceiling from excitement, I suggested, "What about asking Pomona First Federal to join with you in this loan? I was pastor of the First Baptist Church in Pomona. Paul Walker, the president of that organization, is a good friend of mine. He loaned money to me to buy a home while I was in Pomona. He was also always helpful to our church in financial matters. I think he might be interested."

Bob Fuller responded, "I can think of no better organization than this one. I'll contact them."

I replied by saying that I did not want to be controversial in the matter, but I would like the privilege of making that initial contact with Paul Walker. He granted that permission.

After my administrator and I left his office, we drove immediately to Pomona. We had lunch with Paul Walker. We presented our program to him and he responded very favorably. He said, "Of course, I'll have to get my loan committee's permission to do this, but I have some influence with that committee, and I'll use it in your favor."

To make a long story short, these two institutions merged and made the loan of $1,600,000.00. Because of the size of this loan, the trustees did not want to take it upon themselves to make the decision to accept it. Therefore they presented the facts to the church, pointing out that by accepting the loan, we would have the sanctuary that we so desperately needed. As pastor, I was thrilled and excited when the vote was taken in the business meeting, and it was unanimous. By voting in this way, each member of the church was saying, "By faith, let us go forward and do this job that needs to be done."

But this is not the whole story. There are two more intriguing facets to it. First, after we had been building for several months, it became apparent that we had not borrowed sufficient funds to complete the job. With tongue in cheek, I went back to see Bob Fuller to explain this to him. With a twinkle in his eye, he replied, "Paul Walker and I knew that you had not asked for enough in the beginning. We have therefore set aside another $200,000.00 for you. You may have it whenever you need it."

Our church had stepped out on faith, accepted the loan and started to build. God knew that we needed more money than we had asked for and He laid this upon the hearts of Bob Fuller and Paul Walker. When the emergency arose, that money was available. I'm convinced that this was the case because we acted upon the truth that with God all things are possible.

But there's a second facet to it. While we were building the sanctuary, the trustees had an opportunity to buy $350,000.00 worth of additional property. This was property that they knew we were going to need for future development. As they thought and prayed about it, they gave consideration to the fact that we were already $1,800,000.00 in debt. They also realized that we did not have $3.50 to put down on this new venture. However, by faith, they decided to buy it. They were able to work out satisfactory terms with the owners, and we purchased it. We are now using it in our athletic program. By faith, the First Baptist Church in Van Nuys built a new sanctuary and purchased this property.

On March 14, 1965, it was my delight to stand in our pulpit and preach the dedicatory sermon for this new facility. That morning, we dedicated our sanctuary to the preaching and the teaching of the gospel of our Lord Jesus Christ. Through the years, many people

101

have come to know Christ as their Saviour in that facility and for this we praise His Name.

A second evidence that the First Baptist Church in Van Nuys operates on the basis that with God all things are possible is to be seen in the story of our new youth center, the Bennett Youth Complex. One Sunday morning back in 1968, as I was speaking, I looked over the congregation and saw about 1,000 teenagers. The Spirit of God seemed to say to me, "Stop what you're preaching and tell the people that we need a new youth center at the First Baptist Church in Van Nuys."

(In my preparation for preaching, I not only make copious notes, but after I have made them I go over them two or three times out loud in front of a mirror. By so doing, I make the message literally a part of me. I commit it to memory. When I stand in the pulpit it seems to flow smoothly because of the oral preparation that I have put into it.)

As I continued preaching that morning, I was increasingly impressed to yield to the Spirit's leadership. I was actually saying one thing but thinking another and the tension was mounting. When you get into a situation like this, it is most difficult to handle. Finally in desperation, I quit preaching. I looked at the congregation and said, "I have just had an experience in this pulpit, the like of which I have never had before." I'm quite sure some of the people thought that I had a heart attack, and consequently I had their undivided attention. Quickly I assured them that there was nothing physically wrong—that my experience had been a spiritual one. I said, "While I've been delivering the sermon which I prepared this week for you, the Spirit of God has been speaking to my heart. He has asked me to stop preaching my prepared message and simply share with you the fact that we need a new youth center. In my opinion, this project will cost

$1,000,000.00. I have no idea from whence this money will come. As you know, we have an indebtedness of about $1,800,000.00. Only God knows where the additional $1,000,000.00 can be secured. Therefore, I am asking you to pray about it. Pray about it in your personal devotions. Pray about it in your family devotions. We shall pray about it in our corporate prayer meetings here at the church. We don't need this youth center ten years from now. We need it now, for more than 50 percent of the people living in the San Fernando Valley are teenagers or below. Please pray with me about it."

After the service, two of the trustees in our church came to me. These were men of great faith. However, this particular morning, I had stretched that faith out of all proportion. They said, "Pastor, you really blew it today." When I inquired what they meant, they explained, "You told our people in effect that we could have a $1,000,000.00 youth center. They believe what you say from the pulpit. Obviously, we can't get it, and when the people realize this, they're going to lose confidence in you and this will break the high morale of our church. You really blew it."

For a moment I stood there looking at them, saying nothing, and then I inquired, "Aren't you fellows my friends?" When they assured me that they were, I continued. "Don't you believe in prayer?" When they acquiesced to this fact, I said to them, "Will you during this next year withhold judgment? Instead of judging, will you pray with me that the Lord will give us this new youth center?" They agreed to this. Nothing more was said at that time.

That evening before the service one of our college men came to me and said, "Pastor, I'm going to pray about what you said this morning, but I'm also going to act upon it. Here is $15.00 with which to begin the fund." At the evening service that night, I asked our people not to be presumptive and pray that God would give us $1,000,000.00. I said to them, "We don't need that amount. We only need $999,985.00. Just ask Him for this amount." Then I told them the story of what this college boy had done.

This evidently inspired others to follow his example. By the end of the year from the time that I made the announcement, the people had given $20,000.00 in addition to their regular contributions to the church.

But this isn't where the story concludes. Six months before the end of the year, I was playing golf one day with my good friend Al Bennett, who was the president and owner of Liberty Records. After we had completed our game, while we were having lunch together, I asked him, "Al, why don't you give us $1,000,000.00 for our youth center? Your wife and children are active members of our church. They would derive great benefit from it as well as all of our other people."

He answered, "Preacher, I don't have $1,000,000.00."

Laughingly, I said, "Well, Al, while I was out on the golf course, you were telling me how rich you were. You were either telling me a fib there or you're telling me one here. Now which is it? Do you have the money or don't you?"

He replied, "Well I have it, but I don't have it in liquid form." I suggested to him that we could easily liquidate some of his assets and apply the money to the project. He thought for a moment and then responded, "Preacher, I can't do that. But if I ever sell my business, I will give you the $1,000,000.00."

Four weeks before the end of the year, I read in the Los Angeles Times that Liberty Records had been sold to Transamerica for $25,000,000.00.

Do you know what I did? Of course you do. I went to the telephone. I called Al. I congratulated him upon

From the sanctuary (top) to the latest educational unit, (bottom), the building program has proceeded on faith.

the sale. Then I said to him, "Al, don't you and I have something about which to talk?"

He asked, "What do you mean?"

I then reminded him of the conversation that we had at the Bel Air Country Club during lunch. I pointed out to him that he had promised the Lord that he would give the $1,000,000.00 for a youth center if he ever sold his business. He replied, "Preacher, you're right. Come and see me."

Just one year from the day the Lord laid it upon my heart to ask our people to be praying for a youth center, Al and Kathy Bennett were in our sanctuary and they dedicated to the Lord's work $1,000,000.00 in Transamerica stock for the purpose of building this youth center. After this, Transamerica stock began to rise rather rapidly. In discussing with Al how he would give the stock, he suggested that because of the advance of the stock market, he thought that he would be better off from a tax standpoint and our church would be far better off financially, if he would give it over a five year period. Since he was giving the money, naturally I agreed with his suggestion.

We began to operate on this basis. He said to us, "I'm on the Board of Transamerica. We own Occidental Insurance Company. I will make is possible for church to get a loan from Occidental for $1,000,-000.00, with which to build the center. And as the stock advances and you receive it, you can easily pay off the loan and keep the balance above the loan for other projects."

Encouraged by this, we instructed our architect to begin immediately the drawings for this new project. Then we began our negotiations with Occidental for the loan. We found them most cooperative. Progress was rapidly being made for the finalizing of the financial arrangement that Al had suggested to us. At this point something happened. The stock market, instead of going up, began to decline. Occidental, recognizing that this might present some difficult problem, slowed down the processing of the loan. When finally they were ready for us to sign the note, the total value of the stock which Al had given to us was $850,000.00, and it was still going down.

Instead of signing that note, my business manager and I asked for the privilege of having lunch with Al to discuss this matter with him. In the course of our conversation, I pointed out to them that if he continued to give us the stock at the rate he was presently doing, by the time we had it all and cashed it, more than fifty percent of the total proceeds would go to pay off the interest on the note that we had signed. I further called his attention to the fact that this was placing the financial condition of our church in jeopardy. I then asked him to consider giving us at once all of the stock which he promised. Without hesitation he replied that he had been thinking about the situation and was prepared to grant our request.

Within just a matter of a few days, we had more than 33,000 shares of Transamerica in our possession. As we discussed with the trustees what we should do, they were faced with a problem: Should they sell these shares of stock for $850,000.00 and make arrangements for a loan of $150,000 to build the building, or should they hold the stock, believing that ultimately it would come back and pay off all the indebtedness?

They discussed this matter at length. They prayed about it and sincerely and earnestly sought the will of the Almighty concerning their action. Finally, the decision was made. They went with the idea of holding the stock, believing in the American economy and feeling that even if it went down further, ultimately it would

107

make a comeback and take care of all of our debts in the Bennett Youth Complex.

In the meantime, our architect was continuing to draw the plans. When he finalized them and they were accepted by the City Planning Department, we had to face the question as to whether or not we would hold up the building or go full speed ahead. The trustees didn't debate this for a moment. They decided that with God all things are possible, and therefore they would not delay the building even as much as one day. We signed the contract with the Fellows Construction Company of Glendale, California, for the building of this structure.

The story of our financing this building is indeed an intriguing one. We were able to put up our stock for collateral and borrow $350,000.00 from a local bank against it.

The bank told us that if the stock declined to 11%, they would sell it and pay themselves off. God really tested our faith. The stock declined to 11%. When it did, the president of the bank called our business manager and informed him, "This morning we're going to sell the stock and pay off your loan."

The business manager brought him up short. He said, "Don't you dare do that. Our agreement is that you will sell the stock only if it goes to 11%. At the present, it is 11%."

God saw us through this emergency. The stock never went below the 11% point, and the bank did not sell it. But we found that the $350,000.00 was not enough to build a $1,000,000.00 structure. We finally ran out of money.

Once again the trustees had to decide whether we would stop the building or go on by faith, believing that God would provide for our needs. After discussing the matter briefly, their decision was to continue the construction. We began to dig down into our general fund and used as much as we possibly could of that in financing this construction program. By doing this, we actually put our budget in a $70,000.00 deficit position. The Almighty saw us through this crisis in a marvelous way and the day came when we were able to replace these funds needed to operate our program day by day.

When we finally ran out of the funds provided by the general budget, again the trustees had to face the question as to whether to stop the construction or to go on by faith, depending upon the Lord to provide the necessary means. Like the previous two times, they decided to go on with the building.

In order to raise money to meet the monthly payment, I challenged our people during the month of August (probably the worst month in the entire year) to raise money to give as much over and above their regular tithing as they possibly could in order to help us through this emergency.

Our people are great. They're not rich, but they love the Lord. During the month of August they gave an additional $240,000. This money also finally ran out, and we were faced with the necessity of finding another source of funds. Here again, the trustees were called and asked whether or not we should stop the building. Their reply was, "Let's go full speed ahead believing that with God nothing is impossible."

Earle Brookins, one of our trustees, and I called on the president of the Lincoln Bank where our church does its banking. As we sat in his office I said to him, "Jack, how much will you give Earle on his signature?"

He answered, "$50,000.00."

I replied, "Prepare the note. Earle, when it's prepared, you sign it." Then I looked at the president of the bank and inquired, "How much will you give me on my signature?" I thought he would say, $1,000.00

or maybe $2,000.00. He nearly bowled me over when he responded, "$25,000.00." I instructed him to get the note ready, assuring him that I was prepared to sign it. As I was doing so, I told him that if he ever had to collect $25,000.00 from me, he would have to sell me as a slave, but I appreciated his confidence.

We were able to get some other of our men to do as Earle Brookins and I had done, until finally we had raised $220,000.00 by this means and the building continued. However, like the other instances, we finally used up all the $220,000.00, and we needed $236,000.00 more. Where were we going to get this? And if we couldn't get it, should we stop the building? Our trustees by this time had really had their faith tested. They met together to discuss the situation. I was so pleased: Their faith did not waver for even a second. They took the position that God had seen us through thus far and He was not about to let us down at this time. They gave instructions to continue with the program.

We went to our general contractor and discussed our situation with him. He suggested that maybe he had a bank contact that would help. The Lord laid it upon his heart to go to his bank to borrow the money personally to pay himself and his men, with our church guaranteeing the loan. His banker was willing to accept this proposition and so we financed the final $236,000.00 in this manner.

On February 21, 1971, we dedicated this new youth center. We call it the Bennett Youth Complex. And there is more to the story!

The financing that we had arranged on this building was a hodgepodge affair. It was necessary for us to find the money to pay off the various banks from which we borrowed, and to pay the notes of the individuals who had borrowed money for us. We looked all over the San Fernando Valley and the Los Angeles area for a financial institution that would loan us $1,000,000.00 for this construction. We were not successful.

One day I went to see my good friend, Art Aston, who had taken Bob Fuller's place as the president of the San Fernando Valley Federal. I said to him, "Art, you're not very happy with the loan that you have from our church, because of the low interest."

He answered, "You know I'm not happy with it, but what can I do?"

I replied, "You can probably raise the interest if you will accommodate us in another way."

When he asked me what I meant, I explained our situation to him. I emphasized that we needed a $1,000,000.00 loan. I said, "If you would be willing to put the loan that we have with you now with an additional loan of $1,000,000.00 we'll be glad to pay the going rate of interest. We will be helping you, and you will be helping us."

This really appealed to him. He said, "I'll contact the Pomona First Federal to see if they'll go along with it, and if they will, we'll make arrangements for this money."

To make a long story short, on May 18, a $2,500,000.00 loan was granted to us by the San Fernando Valley Federal Savings & Loan Company and Pomona First Federal Savings & Loan Company. This represents the total indebtedness for the buildings that we're using on our present campus.

We still have our Transamerica stock. Because of the dividends that we have received, that stock now amounts to 34,220 shares. We believe that God is going to see us through—that ultimately this original gift will take care of this financial indebtedness.

In the meantime, our people are giving in such a manner that we are able to handle the loan and to increase our program week by week. And we have discovered that the Bennett Youth Complex is a tremendous asset to us as we seek to minister to the teenagers and the college men and women in our community.

Because the First Baptist Church in Van Nuys has experienced it and because the Bible teaches it, each of our members can say with the Angel Gabriel, "With God nothing is impossible."

I love to think of the way in which the writer of the book of Hebrews expresses the power of faith in the very last part of chapter 11. There he writes: *And what more shall I say? For time will fail me if I tell of Gideon, Barak, Samson, Jephthah; of David and Samuel and the prophets; who by faith conquered kingdoms, performed acts of righteousness, obtained promises, shut the mouths of lions, quenched the power of fire, escaped the edge of the sword, from weakness were made strong, became mighty in war, put foreign armies to flight. Women received* back *their dead by resurrection; and others were tortured, not accepting their release, in order that they might obtain a better resurrection; and others experienced mockings and scourgings, yes, also chains and imprisonment. They were stoned, they were sawn in two, they were tempted, they were put to death with the sword; they went about in sheepskins, in goatskins; being destitute, afflicted, ill-treated men of whom the world was not worthy, wandering in deserts and mountains and caves and holes in the ground.*

Because of their faith, God saw them through their difficulties and met their every need.

The other day, one of the seminary students from our church and I were having lunch together. In the course of our conversation, he told me that often in the school year, one of his fellow students will ask him the question, "What is the secret of the growth of the First Baptist Church in Van Nuys?"

After telling me this, he inquired as to what I would say in answer to such a question. I responded, "There are many contributing factors to our growth, but the one thing from the human standpoint that is above all others, is the fact that the laymen of our church really believe that with God all things are possible, and they are willing to act upon this faith."

I have many pastor friends. A number of these men have great vision for their churches. They are men of dedication, of ability and they're Spirit led. They have faith, just as much as I have or perhaps even more. But they are not able to accomplish much because their laymen are lacking in faith. They are like the people in Nazareth about whom the Scripture says, *He* (Jesus) *could do no mighty work there because of their unbelief.*

No pastor can get a job done of any consequence for God, unless he is surrounded by laymen who have faith in the power of God to perform miracles today, just as He did during biblical times. As pastor of the First Baptist Church in Van Nuys, I praise the Name of the Lord for the many, many laymen that we have in our church who have this quality of faith. Without them, my hands would be tied and the church, instead of progressing, would be retrogressing.

CHAPTER 9

Diversified in Service

There is no doubt that the greatest theological treatise ever produced is the Epistle to the Romans. One of the things that greatly impresses me about this particular document is the way in which the apostle Paul begins it. He writes: *Paul, a bond-servant of Christ Jesus, called as an apostle, set apart for the gospel of God, which He promised beforehand through His prophets in the holy Scriptures, concerning His Son, who was born of the seed of David according to the flesh, who was declared with power* to be *the son of God by the resurrection from the dead* (Rom. 1:1-4).

A careful perusal of this statement reveals that the apostle Paul calls attention to the fact that he was a servant, before he mentioned that God had made him an apostle. *Paul, a bond-servant of Christ Jesus, called as an apostle.* The word "bond-servant" means bond slave. First and foremost, the apostle Paul was a bond slave of Jesus Christ. His greatest desire was to do the will of his Saviour.

He echoes this same sentiment in 1 Corinthians 9:19-22. There he writes: *For though I am free from all men, I have made myself a slave to all, that I might win the more. And to the Jews I became as a Jew, that I might win Jews; to those who are under the Law, as under the Law, though not being myself under the Law, that I might win those who are under the Law; to those who are without law, as without law, though not being without the law of God but under the law of Christ, that I might win those who are without law. To the weak I became weak, that I might win the weak; I have become all things to all men, that I may by all means save some.*

The philosophy of the First Baptist Church in Van Nuys is exactly the same as that of the apostle Paul's. We are convinced that first and foremost, we are a service institution. If there is a job that needs to be done in the Name of the Lord Jesus Christ and for His glory, we are convinced that is is incumbent upon us to do that job.

Following this philosophy during the years that I have been privileged to pastor the church, we have greatly enlarged our program. For example, when I first came to this pastorate, the trustees were having a great deal of trouble with the Boy Scouts. In the first trustee meeting that we had, someone suggested that we throw the scouts out of the church and have nothing more to do with the organization. Recognizing the fact that there is a real ministry to boys through scouting, I suggested that we use another method; that instead of throwing them out, that we get behind them, that we provide for them a nice place in which to meet and secure adequate leadership for them.

116

The trustees reluctantly went along with my suggestion. How grateful I am that they did. Today, we have
one of the finest Boy Scout programs than I know anything about. We also have a fine Girl Scout activity.
This has resulted in our not only reaching many boys
and girls, but also in our being able to confront their
parents with the gospel of the Lord Jesus Christ.

About a year ago, we had a potluck supper for the
parents of some of our scouters. Over three hundred
adults attended. Many of these people were not related
to our church in any way. In this informal time, I, as
the pastor, had an opportunity to get acquainted with
them and to invite them to our services. I also had a
chance to speak to the group and in so doing, give a
strong witness for the Saviour.

When I arrived on the scene in Van Nuys, we were
having some difficulty with our bookstore. Dr. Porter
Barrington, the pastor who had preceded me, had seen
a great need in the San Fernando Valley for a facility
in which the best in Christian literature could be made
available to our area. As a result of his vision, the
church had started this particular store. However, our
building which housed it was inadequate. When the
manager became ill, some of our men wanted to close
it. They pointed out that we were losing money—that
perhaps someone who had a better grasp of business
techniques should come and take over the store and
make whatever profit he could out of it, leaving the
church completely free of responsibility.

Once again, as in the case of the scouts, I suggested
to our men that instead of getting rid of it, we do
something about improving it. We did. Today it is one
of the finest facilities of this type in the entire United
States. Although our purpose is to serve the community, not to make money out of it, we are operating in
the black. And God is blessing this ministry. Often-

117

times, so the clerks tell me, people in trouble come in seeking help through Christian reading. This gives them an opportunity not only to present the material that they need, but also witness to them. Many have come to know Jesus Christ as Saviour and Lord as the result of this. Right now we have one major problem. There is such a demand for our products, that the new building occupied by the store is not large enough to take care of the needed inventory. I am sure that within a short time, we will be enlarging this physical facility. As a matter of fact, we have plans on the drawing board for it now.

My ministry in Van Nuys began on the second Sunday in July, 1959. In the fall of that year, we had our first and only every-member canvass. As a result of this, we had a number of inquiries by parents as to when we were going to began an elementary day school. Sensing that there was a real need for this, we began to look into it. Frankly speaking, at the outset, I was against it. I felt that the parochial school system started by Baptists had been initiated because of hostility toward the public schools. Later on, as the result of my research, I was happy to discover that this was not true. As a matter of fact, I found that the public educators in the San Fernando Valley were encouraging all of the churches that could do so, to move in this direction. They needed assistance. The area schools were overcrowded. Often one would hear the remark that every Monday a new elementary school was being opened in the San Fernando Valley.

With the understanding that ours was not a protest school, we began in the fall of 1960 with a kindergarten and three grades. The enrollment for that year was 65. To me it is very significant that 80 percent of the people who put their children into our school were not connected with our church in any way. Many of these were not even believers. Down deep in their hearts, however, they were convinced that their children should have some Christian education. They themselves did not want to become involved in church and Sunday school, so they salved their consciences by sending their children to our day school. This presented us with a tremendous evangelistic opportunity, which we took advantage of that year and have continued to do so throughout the ensuing years.

At the present time our school has a kindergarten and six grades. Our enrollment for this year has been 395. It appears now that our enrollment for next year will be 420. We are able to take care of this increased number because of our Bennett Youth Center.

I maintain, without fear of contradiction, that our school affords children as fine an elementary education as can be had anywhere. We see to it that our classes are no larger than 30. There is great stress put upon the intellectual disciplines. We expect the children to do homework. We demand that they come up to their full potential. They are challenged by the intellectual atmosphere that pervades the classrooms.

We also have a significant spiritual program for the school. We subscribe to the idea that the fear of the Lord is the beginning of wisdom. As the result of this emphasis through the years we have been able to win many of our students to Jesus Christ as Saviour and Lord. We have also reached a number of their parents for the Saviour.

We have a well rounded program for both boys and girls. For example, the public schools in our area no longer have music for their children because of limited budget. Unlike them, we have a very strong department in this area. Every child in our school has the opportunity of learning the fundamentals of music through this curriculum. I must admit that I am a convert to the parochial school movement. I have seen through the years the good that has been accomplished because of it.

Shortly after I arrived in Van Nuys and began to peruse the various activities that were taking place in the church, I discovered that we had a comprehensive program for young people, and in Rev. Royal Blue we had one of the most outstanding youth leaders to be found anywhere in the country. However, nothing was being done for senior citizens. For several years prior to this time, I had been interested in the study of geriatrics. I knew something of the problems of people who were forced to retire and who did not know what to do with their time. As I examined the membership of our church, I discovered that we had many in this category. Right then and there I decided that we must do as much for them as we were doing for our youth. I announced in the church that those who were interested in starting a senior citizens' program were to meet on the following Tuesday night. There were 12 who attended this initial meeting. They were enthusiastic about the potential for developing a program for their age group. That night they named their group "the Jolly Sixties." That was more than 11 years ago. Since that time, this program has developed in an unbelievable manner. Altogether we have on our rolls more than 800 participating members.

The program is basically threefold: spiritual, social and service. It is spiritual in that we have an adult Sunday school department and a weekly Bible class for this group. In addition, every Friday morning following the Bible class, the group engage in a visitation and witnessing outreach in behalf of the church. Through this many of these senior citizens have developed into effective soul winners. Theirs is a real Jesus movement.

The social part of the program consists of three activities: First, a monthly party, at which we have an attendance of somewhere between 350 and 450. Second, a monthly bus trip to one of the scenic spots in Southern California; and third, about every three or four years, a trip to a place like the Hawaiian Islands or Alaska. As of this moment, while I am writing this chapter, 33 of our Jolly Sixties are enjoying a cruise through the inland waterways of Alaska.

One of the most interesting results of the social aspects of this program is that, to some extent at least, the Jolly Sixties have become a matrimonial bureau. We have had many marriages develop because of it.

It is intriguing to me that when a Jolly Sixties couple falls in love and decides to get married, they want to go through the same procedure as our young couples do in preparation for marriage. For example, they insist on premarital counseling. When they come to me for this session, I limit the discussion to their answer to this one question: "What are you going to do with your money when you get married?"

Inevitably, they will raise their eyebrows at this as they reply, "Pastor, what on earth do you mean by this? What does this have to do with our getting married?"

I will look at her and say, "Don't you have children?"

If she responds in the affirmative, I continue, "Don't you want your money to go to your children at your death?" And inevitably her answer is "yes." Then I will look at him and ask him the same questions. Then I explain to them that they have to settle the issue of money before they get married for if they don't, they will find themselves in big trouble. I then demand that they write up an agreement between themselves as to how they're going to handle their

121

money after they're married. I assure them that after each of them has signed that agreement, I will proceed with the wedding ceremony.

In the early days of the Jolly Sixties, we had one or two sad cases, marriages that ended in failure, simply because the couples did not resolve their problem prior to the exchanging of their wedding vows.

Yes, the program of the Jolly Sixties is spiritual; it is social and it is also service. For example, all the meals that are served in our church are prepared by our caterer and served by our Jolly Sixties. We have a group from this organization that comes to our office every Friday and folds the bulletins. When we have inserts to put into the bulletins, they take care of this matter also. Practically all of the bulk mailing that goes out of our office is handled by them. And in addition to all of this, they have three splendid musical organizations, a singing choir, a melodic choir and a harmonica choir. Oftentimes on a Sunday night, these three choirs go out together under the leadership of the director of the Jolly Sixties, Mr. Dave MacKerron, and conduct services for other churches. The reports that come back to us are always glowing. The pastors are quick to let me know of their deep appreciation for our sending the Jolly Sixties to them.

These wonderful people literally give hundreds, yes, thousands of man hours in our church in serving Jesus Christ. It would be impossible because of the limitation of budget for us to pay for the services they give. I thank God for them. Without hesitation, I recommend to every church that they put on a similar program. It does not cost one dime, and the dividends that accrue to the church are immeasurable.

One of the great needs that we find among our senior citizens is that of adequate housing, especially housing that is close to the church. Many of these people are no longer able to drive because of impaired vision or some other physical problem. They have a desire to live close to the church so that they can take part in the activities of the Jolly Sixties.

For a number of years we have been negotiating for a loan with which to build a senior citizens' complex. This year we received word that our application had been approved and that money would be set aside for the construction of the senior citizens' complex.

The Lord willing, and I am sure that He is, within two years we will have completed a 196 unit, ten-story senior citizens' apartment house. Right now our Jolly Sixties are lining up, making application for residence therein. This complex will meet a tremendous need.

Here in the San Fernando Valley we have a number of husbands and wives who are gainfully employed in business. This creates a problem for them as to what they're going to do with their children during the working hours. While school is on, this problem is not so acute as it is in the summertime. Eleven years ago, our church, realizing that something needed to be done to assist these parents in solving their problems, began a day camp. For about $18.00 per week, mother and dad can put junior into the day camp where he will have a well-rounded program of horseback riding, swimming, softball, surfing, handicraft, Bible study and once a week a trip to Disneyland.

In addition to solving the problem for working parents in the summertime, this day camp also affords the church an opportunity of furnishing summer employment for their dedicated school teachers and for many of our college students. These people are really servants of Christ. They take full advantage of the opportunity they have in the day camp, sharing their faith with the boys and girls. A great many decisions have been made for Christ as a result of this.

I remember one day last summer walking across the campus of our church, when suddenly I heard someone calling my name. I turned around and saw that one of our day camp leaders was running toward me. When he reached me I could see that he was excited. He said, "Pastor, I led chapel in the day camp today. When I gave the invitation, eighteen boys and girls accepted Christ as their Saviour." Then he went on to point out that he was going to contact their parents to share with them what their children had done and seek to lead them to make a similar decision. Every year since the day camp has been in operation, we have broken even financially and in some years we've done even a little better than that. And great spiritual dividends have accrued to the cause of Christ because of it.

Our music program is another great avenue of service for Christ in the church. It has contributed much to the development of our overall program. Fifteen years ago, when our present minister of music, Dr. John Gustafson, began his ministry, there were two choirs, with a total enrollment of about 150. Today, there are 36 choirs, with 1,800 people participating. These individuals are not only serving Christ through singing, but many of them are contributing to the well-being of our church by their participation in the actual administration of these musical groups. For example, in our children's program we have 90 volunteers who organize, promote, administer and lead their choirs.

Because of the rapid expansion of the overall music ministry, we have had to add personnel to our professional staff. At the present time, we have seven people in the employ of this department. In addition to the director, there are assistant directors, two full time secretaries, an organist and a pianist. An entire book could be written just on the undertakings and accomplishments of our ministry of music.

Let me just call to your attention two or three of the highlights. For example, every year at Christmas, there are two outstanding presentations. The first is made by our great Amen Choir, which is our senior group. On Sunday night, two weeks before Christmas they present a program entitled "Carols by Candlelight." In this presentation, they sing the melodius Yuletide music, accompanied not only by our organ and piano, but also by an excellent symphony orchestra. The narration for it is done in stereophonic sound by some outstanding radio and TV personality. Each year, as the choir sings the story of Christ's nativity, those who are in the audience feel as if they are in the very presence of the Lord Jesus Himself. The beauty of this is indescribable. As they leave the sanctuary, they are spiritually uplifted and inspired, filled with awe and reverence for the King of kings and Lord of lords.

Also, during this season, our College Career Choir presents the Living Christmas Tree. We have what we laughingly call the world's largest Tinker Toy. It is actually a tree made out of steel which we superimpose over our choir loft. It is able to accommodate 150 singers in its branches. It is decorated with green boughs, lights and simulated snow. The choir members become the ornaments on the tree by wearing red dickies. Because of the public demand, admission to these performances is by ticket only. They are made available without charge through the church office. This procedure enables us to regulate the number attending each performance thereby keeping the fire department off our back. Last year we had eight presentations. This coming year, nine are scheduled. I am sure that if time permitted and our young people were up to it physically, we could fill our sanctuary at least thirty times with this program.

In 1970, our 175 voice High School Choir had the

privilege of doing the West Coast premiere of Otis Skilling's musical, "Life." They presented it again in 1971 on two consecutive Sunday nights, and the Lord saw fit to bless with 198 decisions being made for Christ and the church.

In 1970, our College Career Choir presented the West Coast premiere of Ralph Carmichael's "Tell It Like It Is," and during 1971 had the privilege of doing the West Coast premiere of Kurt Kaiser's and Ralph Carmichael's "Natural High." They repeated this and as a result there were many decisions made for the Saviour.

Our ministry of music stays current in its program. It is the intention of this department to present all of the good new Christian musicals that are being written. Our entire church is convinced that this is the new mood of evangelism. God is using this method to win many precious souls for the Lord Jesus Christ and we are anxious to be in on this.

Through the years as our membership has grown, the need for pastoral ministries has become more and more acute. In order to meet this need, we have developed an entire department of practical care. This department, headed by Rev. Ed Kriz, now has in it three full time men, plus one part time man. We have an answering service. One pastor is on call at all times. Through this avenue, pastoral care is available to our people 24-hours a day, 7-days a week. We find that this service is deeply appreciated by our membership and is constantly being used.

One Sunday about 10 years ago, a lady came up to me and asked, "Pastor, why don't we have a program for deaf people like my father and mother? As far as I know, there is no spiritual ministry for these people in the entire San Fernando Valley."

I responded by inquiring, "Are you able to sign?" When she answered in the affirmative, I said, "We will

begin the deaf program next Sunday. I will set aside a
section in the sanctuary for deaf people. You get in
touch with as many of them as you possibly can and invite them to come to the service. You be there with
them, prepared to interpret my sermon for them." She
accepted this challenge, and our deaf program began in
this manner.

At the present time, we have a full program for this
group. We are ministering to more than 150. We have
four deaf deacons. We have a full time secretary, Mrs.
Elmyra Lam, in the department and, because we have
recently lost our pastor to the deaf, we are seeking a
new one. We believe in God's own time He will send
the right man to us. In the meantime, with the assistance of the members of our pastoral care department
and with our secretary, who is literally a director of the
department, we are enlarging this ministry.

Shortly after we organized our deaf department,
someone came and inquired about the blind, stating,
"Pastor, if you'll look at the ministry of our Lord Jesus
Christ, you will discover that not only did He minister
to the deaf but also to the blind. Why don't we do
something for the sightless people who stand in real
need of assistance?" I asked that person if he would assist in doing this, and he said, "Yes." We began the
blind program immediately. God has seen fit to bless
this in a remarkable way. We have 20 to 30 blind people who are regularly attending our services. We have
a social program, a recreational program and a spiritual
program for them.

For example, we have five bowling teams among the
blind. Brunswick has developed a banister that can be
put on the side of the alley. A blind person can hold on
to that banister with his left hand, hold the bowling
ball in his right hand, walk down the alley and, when
his left hand hits a certain spot on the banister, he

knows to let the ball go. Our blind have a delightful time in this activity.

Because we care, we have been able to lead a number of these to Jesus Christ. Each time one comes forward to make a decision for the Saviour, I always say something like this to the congregation: "This morning, we are happy that Mr. So-and-So is making his decision for Jesus Christ. Even though he cannot see with his eyes, he is able to see with his heart that God loves him and has provided redemption for him in Christ Jesus. On this basis, he comes forward today to acknowledge Christ as his Saviour and his Lord."

There is another interesting facet to the blind program that is of great import to the church. Obviously, the Department of Motor Vehicles in the State of California cannot issue drivers' licenses to those who cannot see. In order to get these handicapped persons to and from the church and to and from their various activities, it is necessary for us to have sighted people to drive them—people who are willing to give their time and talents in serving Christ in this way. Whenever someone says to me, "Pastor, I would like to serve the Lord but I can think of nothing I can do for Him. I am unable to sing. I don't have a voice for this. I cannot teach a Sunday school class because my biblical knowledge is limited. But if there was some way I could serve Him, I would sure do it." I immediately respond, "There is a way that you can serve Him. Can you drive a car?" Inevitably the answer is "yes." And then I tell this person about our need for drivers of the blind. In our church at the present time we have over 100 people who are transporting their sightless brothers and sisters to the various services and activities in which they are involved.

One of the happiest nights of the year for me is the night we have our annual banquet for these drivers. On

To meet the needs of the people, a ministry to deaf, a
day school and a creative music program are conducted.

this occasion I have the opportunity of personally thanking these people for literally giving hundreds of hours in transporting those who cannot see. I point out to them that by their willingness to do this, they are making it possible for blind people to enjoy Christian fellowship and to have the opportunity of worshiping the Lord together with their fellow Christians in the church. I am sure that each one who is having a part in this driving program is receiving great personal satisfaction from it. I have had many thank me for this opportunity because of the happiness it has brought to them.

Oftentimes in the church, the shut-ins are a forgotten group. "Out of sight—out of mind" is often the case, as far as they are concerned. This is not true in our church, however. We have an extension department which takes care of these people. It is under the direction of Mrs. Olive Sorvig, a part time staff member, who makes sure that every shut-in is called on at least once a month. The caller takes good Christian literature into the home and has a time of prayer and Bible study with the person. In addition to this, our deacons, once a month, serve communion to each of our shut-ins. Once a year, on the first Sunday in June, we do our best to provide transportation for all shut-ins who are ambulatory so that they can attend the church service. Usually we have over 100 of these, who are our special guests at the 11 A.M. communion service. Following this, we have a luncheon for them. At this luncheon it is my privilege to speak to them and then to get acquainted with them personally. All of our shut-ins, as a result of this program, feel they are an integral part of the church. Many of them are our faithful supporters not only in their prayers, but with their finances as well.

Newborn babies are a center of interest, not only

for their mothers and dads and their grandparents, but also for our church. We have a cradle roll department under the direction of Mrs. Helen Jackson, a very competent person. When a baby is born, the parents are visited by this cradle roll director. She has classes for the mothers on how to rear their children in the nurture and in the admonition of the Lord. She spends many hours in the homes of these babies, counseling with the mothers and dads concerning their need of putting Jesus Christ first in their relationship. God is using her ministry in a marvelous way to bring families closer together, to unite them in Jesus Christ and to cause them to grow in their spiritual lives through the establishing of family altars and through their involvement in serving Christ in the church.

She has developed a tremendous follow-up program that is geared to meet the needs of new converts in her department. This program consists of eight hours of Bible lessons which are available to the new convert. When a mother or dad in her department accepts Christ as Saviour, she sends one of her trained workers into the home to meet with the person on a one-to-one basis. For eight consecutive weeks, one hour per week, this one-to-one meeting takes place. During this time, the trained worker teaches the basic truths of Christianity. This enables the convert to grow in grace and in the knowledge of our Lord and Saviour Jesus Christ, right at the beginning of his Christian experience. It usually results in two things: First, the new convert becomes established in the faith; and second, he becomes a volunteer to go and teach some other new convert what he has learned. My staff and I are so impressed by this program that we are adopting it for our entire church.

Just recently, the deaf program, the blind program, the extension program and the cradle roll program have been organized into a department which we call the Department of Special Ministries. This is being administered by Rev. Dale Scott who is one of our pastors. I am sure that by his coordinating of this work, we are going to do a more effective job for our Lord.

It has long been recognized by evangelical Christians that one of the most effective ways of reaching people with the gospel and with the claims of Christ upon their lives for Christian service is through a camping program. Long before I became the pastor of the First Baptist Church in Van Nuys, this church had this conviction. Under the leadership of my predecessor a lovely camp at Lake Arrowhead was purchased. Through the years, this camp, known as Arrow Pines, has been developed until now it can accommodate 250.

During the past two years, however, the area where Arrow Pines is located has become so commercialized that we have decided we should move our camp elsewhere. We have purchased new property at Frazier Park. As of the moment, we are in the process of selling Arrow Pines and we are anticipating the construction of our new camp just as soon as possible.

In the meantime, we are renting camping facilities in other places and going full speed ahead with this program. This is resulting in many first time decisions for the Saviour. Also, young people are hearing the call of God to full time service. In the future these will be actively serving on the mission fields, in the pastorates, in Christian education, in the ministry of youth or as ministers of music.

Like everything else in our church, our missions department has greatly expanded. The budget is now of such proportions that it is necessary for us to have a full time administrator. God has been good to us in giving us a woman, Mrs. Katherine Coward, who not only understands missions, but also has tremendous organizational ability. She administers our entire missionary program. Each year, the trustees allocate a certain amount of our budget to the Missions Board. It is the responsibility of this board to decide where the money is to be used. They recognize that our administrator is both sensitive to the leadership of the Holy Spirit and to the great missionary needs of the world. They therefore wisely follow her guidance and counsel. I am convinced that the membership of the First Baptist Church in Van Nuys gets as much mileage out of their missionary dollar as any group of people anywhere in evangelical Christianity.

Up until about eight years ago, our church had a typical Men's Brotherhood. By that I mean the men of the church were supposed to meet once a month for a dinner and a program. Each month it became increasingly difficult to get something that would draw our men to the meeting. Promoting this became an arduous task for all who were involved. Supposedly, this brotherhood was to furnish an opportunity of Christian fellowship for our men. Actually, it was furnishing frustration for the leadership. The matter of Christian fellowship was being beautifully handled through the social activities of the organized adult Sunday school classes.

Finally all of us awakened to the reality of the situation and blew the whistle on the program. We eliminated the Men's Brotherhood. We replaced it with the Men's Council, composed of twelve men. It is the responsibility of these leaders to provide activities in which various members of the families can get together for a time of social activity and recreation. Each year, this Council sponsors five golf tournaments, three or four family nights at the ball game, two or three nights in the gym for fathers and daughters and fathers and sons and sponsors an overnight camping trip for fathers and sons. It also promotes several deep sea fishing trips each year. Through the activity of this Men's Council, families are learning that it is really fun to play together and to fellowship together. The council is meeting a real need. I would not go back to the old method of the Men's Brotherhood for anything in the world. As far as I'm concerned, it is for the birds, and they can have it.

In this complex age of which you and I are a part, there is often a need for in-depth counseling by one who is competent both in theology and psychology. I recognize the fact that I am not a good counselor. I am not trained in the field of psychology. However, I appreciate the need for this type of service. Many people were coming to me at the beginning of my ministry seeking counsel from me. I found often that I was over my head and needed to refer them to someone else. Finally, I suggested that we add to our staff a competent counselor to handle these cases. We called a man on a part time basis whom we thought had all of the qualifications. He had written several text books on the subject. He was rather popular as a lecturer in the field. He had served in the school district as a counselor. We were sure that this was the right man.

However, we discovered that we had made a mistake. One day, we were visited by someone from the state government, telling us that we were being threatened with a suit. When we inquired as to why, he went on to point out that a certain person had come to our psychologist for counseling. This individual had not been satisfied with what the counselor said and so she decided to look up his credentials. She discovered that his doctorate was a bogus degree. She also found out that he was not licensed by the State of California as a psychologist, and we had advertised him to be this. The state official informed us that we were guilty of misrepresentation and that our good name was in jeopardy. We were most fortunate in being able to get out of this without any difficulty. The woman finally decided to drop the suit and so we were spared public embarrassment. However, from that time on, we decided that whenever we called a psychologist, we were going to check him out more thoroughly than we had this one. This we have done.

We now have a wonderful department of counseling. We have five licensed counselors. All of these men have advanced degrees; two have their Ph.D. This department, in my opinion, is second to none as far as being able to handle the problems of people today from the standpoint both of theology and psychology. I am grateful for its ministry.

In setting up the department, there was one thing I had to learn. I wanted to make the service of the department free to anyone. Those, however, who were more knowledgeable in the field than I, assured me that this would be a sad mistake—that even if a very minimal charge was made, the people who were receiving the counseling would get more out of it by paying that charge. Finally I yielded to the thinking of others, and we now have a fee schedule which we expect people to follow. Most of them do, and results are good.

One of our families was having difficulty with a high school girl. She was not cooperating. When the girl was brought to our counselor he said to her, "You're going to have to pay me $2.00 out of your allowance for this session." The girl, because of this charge, really listened to what the man had to say and followed his instructions. She told her dad later, "I think I've learned all I need to learn. I don't need to go back there again." The father, in telling me about it, said, "She really did learn her lesson. The fact that she had to pay the $2.00 for that session really made her think. It also motivated her to take full advantage of what she had learned. The situation in our home is much more pleasant now."

This counseling department is meeting a real need, not only in our church but in the entire San Fernando Valley. People from all walks of life and from varying backgrounds are taking advantage of these services. The demand is so great that it is almost impossible for our counselors to take care of all who want to see them. It will not be long, I am sure, until we will be adding more personnel.

Nearly a year ago, while I was preaching one Sunday morning, I said to the congregation, "I am convinced that if Jesus Christ was here, He would have a ministry to those that are victimized by narcotics. I am sure that the Lord wants us to have such a ministry. The only reason we haven't moved ahead on it is because of the lack of budget. I want you to be praying about it, for I feel sure that the need for this type of ministry is so acute in the San Fernando Valley that the First Baptist Church in Van Nuys must do what it can to meet it."

That afternoon a young man called me, inquiring, "Pastor, how much money do you need to get this program started?"

I knew him. I didn't feel that he had a great deal of money and so I asked, "How much do you have?"

He replied, "Would $20,000.00 be sufficient to get the program underway?"

I said, "Man, if you'll give us that kind of money, we'll begin the program tomorrow."

He promised, "I will commit myself to this. You begin the program."

That afternoon, I got in touch with Thom Piper, a young man who had been a gang leader, but who had never used dope himself. Members of his gang had. He

136

therefore knew how to deal with it. He had been thoroughly converted as a result of being at one of our church camps. I asked him if he would like to undertake this ministry. His answer was in the affirmative. On his own, he had been doing it anyway. Now, he could quit his job in the studios and serve the Lord by ministering to those that were hooked on narcotics. He began what is known in our church as the FAM Program which means "For All Mankind." As a result of this program, at least 150 have gotten off of dope. Many have been prevented from getting on it. Some of the things that have taken place as the result of this young man's ministry are miraculous. Let me share one of these with you.

There was a boy by the name of Mark, who came to the FAM Program. He had tried every known type of narcotic. He was really hooked on the stuff. Mark came to know the Lord Jesus Christ and was delivered from this slavery. Immediately, he was really turned on for the Saviour. I baptized his brother about three months after I baptized Mark. I talked to him at the baptismal service, asking him, "Did you ever get on dope like Mark?"

He answered, "Man, he turned me on to dope." But he then added, "When he found Jesus, he turned me on to Him, and I am really happy tonight."

Mark is the leader in one of the local high schools here in the San Fernando Valley. About four months ago, he and two or three of his friends who are really Jesus people went to see the principal of their school. They asked for permission to start a Jesus club on the campus. Because of the recent rulings of the Supreme Court, the principal was apprehensive about giving an affirmative answer. He told him, however, that he would allow him to conduct Jesus meetings on the campus during the nutrition period each day. He said,

"After all, what you talk about on the campus is your business. You have a perfect right to say anything which comes into your mind."

Mark and his friends began a Jesus movement on that campus at the next nutrition period. This has been going on for more than three months. About 180 to 250 young people gather together on that campus each day and talk about Jesus Christ. This has resulted in many kids being introduced to the FAM Program, and as a consequence, they have found Christ, who has delivered them from the use of narcotics.

Recently, a history professor (of Jewish background) in the school was so impressed by what he had seen in Mark, that he invited him to speak to his history class. He gave him the opportunity of taking the entire period and using the time any way he saw fit. For 45 minutes Mark spoke on the subject, "The Bible—Fact or Fiction?" In his presentation he shared the four spiritual laws with the members of his class and strongly advised each one of them who had not done so already to turn on to Jesus Christ.

When the period was over, the Jewish professor came to him and commented, "I don't believe like you do, Mark, but I want to tell you, you have something that I don't have, and I really need it." In telling me about it, Mark said, "I made an office appointment with this professor. I'm counting on you to be praying for me as I try to win him to the Saviour."

There is no doubt about it, the FAM Program is meeting a real need. There is something in connection with it, however, that most of our members don't know. The young man who promised the $20,000.00 actually gave us only $1,000.00. He had every intention of supplying the remaining $19,000.00, but, his investments were in the stock market. When that declined he had to go into bankruptcy. When I discussed this matter with our trustees, even though we didn't have the budget to carry on the program, we felt that it was doing such a job for God in the San Fernando Valley, that we should go ahead with it anyway, trusting that the finances would be forthcoming. And do you know something? They have, and I'm convinced they will continue to do so.

Two months ago, we organized a new corporation which we call the Shepherd's House. Under this one corporation, we have put our counseling service, our FAM program and the coffeehouse. We are intending to add to this as opportunity presents itself a free clinic, a halfway house and a center for the distribution of literature concerning narcotics. On the board of the Shepherd's House we have included not only members of our own church, but fine evangelical Christians of other denominations. In doing this, it is our desire to broaden our base and to be of greater service to our entire community.

With the rapidly advancing program that our church was undertaking, several years ago our men recognized that it was imperative that we get a business administrator who really knew what he was doing. We were fortunate to secure the services of Mr. Ed Welge, who had been eminently successful in the insurance business. Through the years he has served with us, he has been an invaluable addition to our staff. By his wise counsel and guidance we have been able to make the most of every dollar we receive. He has developed a full department since his coming. He now has an assistant business administrator, a comptroller, a bookkeeper, a clerk and a secretary. He is adding a new dimension to his program, that of "deferred giving." He himself will be heading this, turning over many of the responsibilities of the day-by-day work routines to Rev. Whitey Norberg, whose title has been changed from assistant business administrator to business manager. With Mr. Welge directing our Deferred Giving Program, I am confident we will have additional funds with which to develop programs to meet new needs as they arise.

Our philosophy is this: Wherever there is a need, it is the responsibility of our church to meet that need to the glory of God. We have operated on this basis, we are operating on this basis now and, the Lord willing, we shall continue to operate on it until Jesus comes.

CHAPTER 10

Balanced on Emphases

A careful study of American ecclesiology reveals that through the years, two philosophies have been advanced for building a church. Each of these philosophies, if properly implemented, will obtain the desired result. One will do so on a temporary basis, while the other will do so on a more permanent basis.

The first of these philosophies takes the position that a great church is to be built around a preacher. According to this theory, if a man can be found who is a profound thinker, an erudite scholar and a scintillating speaker to occupy the pulpit, a tremendous church organization can be built around his pulpit ministry. And this can be done, but only on a temporary basis. The reason? As soon as this man passes off the scene, the church is hard put to find another pastor equally qualified to take his place. If the church fails to come up with such an individual, then inevitably it will decline.

The second philosophy takes the position that preaching is important, but also that Christian education must be brought into focus with it. It is not a matter of preaching *or* Christian education, but it is a matter of both preaching and Christian education which results in the building of a great church. The Christian education program of such a church centers in the Sunday school. I am convinced that Robert Raikes was inspired of God when he was led to initiate what we know today as the modern Sunday school movement. Again and again, I have said to our church, "It is impossible to build a great church organization of an enduring nature without building a great teaching program through the Sunday school. The church that builds in this way not only builds a great church while a certain pastor occupies the pulpit, but the greatness of that church endures after the pastor has departed and another has been called to take his place."

Let me illustrate these two philosophies for you by summarizing the histories of two Baptist churches, the First Baptist Church in New York City and the First Baptist Church in Dallas, Texas.

During the early 1900s, Dr. I. M. Haldeman was the pastor of the First Baptist Church in New York. This man was a pulpiteer par excellence, a profound prophetic scholar and a prolific writer. That church, during his ministry was one of the truly great ecclesiastical centers in our country. My father was a member of it while he was attending Columbia University. I have often talked with him about his experience there. He told me that people would line up for blocks, waiting to get a seat to hear Dr. Haldeman preach. The entire program was centered around his ministry. They had no Sunday school program to amount to anything.

There was no other type of Christian education outreach that had any punch to it. The entire activity of the church centered in the preaching of Dr. Haldeman. As long as he lived, and occupied the pulpit, the First Baptist Church in New York City had a tremendous influence for God and for good, not only in the Metropolitan area where it was located, but throughout the entire nation.

When Dr. Haldeman died, however, the First Baptist Church in New York could not find a pastor of equal caliber to take his place. Since his departure, that church has consistently declined. The other day I was talking to two friends of mine from New York City. Both of these men are knowledgeable as to what is going on as far as Evangelical Christianity is concerned in that area. They spoke of the First Baptist Church and said that it is only a skeleton of its former self. If you were to attend a Sunday morning service there, you would find a rather small congregation. They no longer have a Dr. Haldeman. They did not have a Christian educational program as one of the bases for the organization; perhaps that is one reason the church has gone so far down hill and has very little influence in the community where it is located.

Now contrast this story with that of the First Baptist Church in Dallas. I lived in Texas during the heyday of Dr. George W. Truett, one of the greatest pulpiteers that ever lived. For 40 years he served the First Baptist Church in Dallas as its pastor. I remember that when he came to the declining years of his ministry, there were many people who predicted that the church would die just as soon as Dr. Truett departed the scene. Wherever one went in Texas and talked to someone who belonged to it, inevitably that person would say, "I am a member of Dr. Truett's church," not, "I am a member of the First Baptist Church in

143

Dallas." Because of this, there were many prognosticators who really believed that its demise would be its fate following the resignation of Dr. Truett. What these prophets of doom failed to see was the fact that Dr. George W. Truett had an appreciation not only for the pulpit ministry, but he also recognized the value and importance of Christian education.

All the while he was developing his preaching ministry, he had a man on his staff by the name of Bob Coleman, who was building a strong Christian education program. The First Baptist Church in Dallas had the largest Sunday school in the South, and it was constantly growing. When Dr. Truett died, the Christian educational program of the church held the people together until the church could call a new pastor.

They found a young man in Oklahoma by the name of Wally A. Criswell. More than 25 years ago he came to that pastorate. Because of the Christian education foundation that Dr. Truett had left, Dr. Criswell has been able to build a superstructure that goes way beyond anything Dr. Truett had there even in his heyday. The accomplishments of this institution have been and are miraculous.

If you were to attend the First Baptist Church in Dallas on a Sunday, you would find that the mammoth sanctuary is filled both at 8:15 and 11 o'clock and again at the Sunday evening service. You would also discover more than 5,000 people in the Sunday school. If you looked at the budget you would be overwhelmed by the fact that the church takes in more than $3 million a year. All of this money is used in advancing the cause of Jesus Christ both at home and abroad.

The First Baptist Church in Dallas was a great church under the ministry of Dr. Truett. The First Baptist Church in Dallas is a greater church under the ministry of Dr. Criswell. And the secret is great preaching, plus a sound Christian education program.

In comparing the two churches, there may be a tendency on the part of some to say, "The First Baptist Church in New York City is a downtown church. Its location is against it. Perhaps this is the factor that has contributed more to its demise than a lack of Christian education." Before you conclusively accept that as fact, let me point out that the First Baptist Church in Dallas is also located in the downtown area. Actually, it is right on the edge of what might be called a ghetto. If you were to look for the worst place in Dallas to put the First Baptist Church, you couldn't find one more suitable to that description than its present location. In addition to this, there are hundreds of fine Baptist churches in the same city that are doing a good job for God. People who attend the First Baptist Church have to drive past many of these other Baptist churches in order to get to it. They do so because of the program that the First Baptist Church in Dallas offers them and the preaching which they hear there. The secret is, and make no mistake about it, good preaching plus a sound Christian education program. Location has very little to do with it.

In the First Baptist Church in Van Nuys, we seek to have this twofold emphasis—sound preaching and effective Christian education. In preparing for my pulpit ministry, I make an effort to spend 20- to 30-hours per week in the study. I have the profound conviction that a man who stands behind a sacred desk and speaks for God must be thoroughly prepared to do so by study and prayer. His number one responsibility is to be ready to share God's message with the people. This principle applies to the Sunday evening message as well as the Sunday morning message. It also applies to the Wednesday evening Bible study. There must be no neglect on the part of the preacher, as far as any one of these messages is concerned, if he is to have God's imprimatur and blessing upon his pulpit ministry.

There is biblical precedence for this modus operandi. In the book of Acts we have the story of the Grecian widows complaining against the Hebrew widows because they were not receiving as much of the social service funds as they thought they should. This problem was taken to the apostles who were asked to settle the issue. The answer that was given is found in Acts 6:3-4. These verses read, *But select from among you, brethren, seven men of good reputation, full of the Spirit and of wisdom, whom we may put in charge of this task. But we will devote ourselves to prayer, and to the ministry of the word.*

The prime responsibility of the pastor of the church is to give himself continually to prayer and to the ministry of the word. In doing this, however, he dare not overlook the Christian education program. Instead, he should recognize that this program is a must if his church is going to continue growing after he has gone. Recognizing the truth of this, in our church we are doing the best we can to build a strong Sunday school program, and God is blessing our efforts. We have had a phenomenal growth during the past few years.

There are six factors that contribute to this. In the first place, we use the coordinator system in the organizational structure. In this particular system, we do not have a general Sunday school superintendent. Instead, we have a general division director of the adult division, Mr. Gene Tripp; a director of the college division, Bob Griffin; the high school division director, Jim Grindle; the junior high school division director, Mike Crooker; and the elementary division director, Alberta Hansen. We have two assistants to our general director in the college division, two in the high school division, one in the junior high school division and four in the elementary division. All of these are paid staff members. The general division directors are on a full time basis and the assistants are on a part time basis.

This has not always been true, however. Long before our church had the budget for this number of staff members in our Christian education department, we followed the coordinator system. At that time we were successful in getting people to volunteer to take the general division directorships. However, as the Sunday school grew and each of these jobs became full time propositions, the income increased, and we were able to employ the necessary personnel to take these responsibilities.

Each of the general division directors is responsible for coordinating all of the Christian education work in his division. Basically, this involves the director in the area of Sunday school, the Sunday night training period, in teacher enlistment and teacher training. The general division directors and their assistants are answerable to our director of Christian education, Mr. Charles Smith, who coordinates this overall program.

The advantage of the coordinator system over the old system, in which a general superintendent ran the entire Sunday school, should be obvious to all. The advantage is at the point of the division of labor. Under the old system, we asked a Sunday school superintendent to do the impossible. He was responsible for everything that took place in the Sunday school. Usually, he was an individual who had to work for a living. Inevitably, because the demands of the Sunday school were too much for him, he would follow one of two courses of action. He would either become so frustrated by his responsibilities that he would quit, or he would decide that he could not do a thorough job anyway, so he would just roll with the tide, getting very little done. In this coordinating system, the labor is divided among various individuals who are highly trained in their particular area. A Sunday school that uses this system has a tremendous advantage over one that harks back to the old system.

The second factor that is contributive to the growth of our Sunday school is the ability of our general division directors to develop a strong faculty. A year ago, I was talking to an outstanding Christian educator of one of the leading Evangelical denominations in the United States. In the course of the conversation, I said to him, "I noticed just recently that the statistics in Sunday school for your denomination show that there is a decline this year. How do you account for this? Why is it that your Sunday school is retrogressing rather than progressing?" Quick as a flash, he answered, "Poor teaching." It is true that if a Sunday school is going to develop and do the job that God wants done, it is necessary that it be staffed with well trained teachers.

Our division directors put a tremendous emphasis upon this phase of our program. We have three basic types of teacher training. On Sunday night, before the evening service, we have a perennial training session. When a general division director enlists a new teacher, he can put that teacher immediately into this program where he or she will receive invaluable help.

In the fall of the year, we have an intensive teacher training school that usually lasts from three to five days. In this school, we bring as our faculty, leading Christian educators in every division of work. We encourage all of our teachers in each division to take advantage of this training. We find this to be most invaluable. These educators come to us. They are conversant with the latest methods in teaching and are able to share these with our people.

"It is impossible to build an enduring church organization without building a great teaching program."

Also, each summer we send between 25 and 35 of our teachers to the Glorietta Encampment in New Mexico for Sunday School week. There they have fellowship with teachers in their division from other churches throughout the United States. They also have the opportunity of hearing the finest Christian educators in the world. They are privileged to see demonstrations of how teaching should be done. They always come back to us with new vim and enthusiasm, ready to go to work for the Lord. I know that even though this costs our church about $3,000.00 per year, it is a good investment. For we realize that a strong faculty inevitably results in a growing Sunday school.

A third factor that has played a prominent part in the growth of our Sunday school is the emphasis we put upon the necessity of consistently contacting absentees. We believe that tact is important, but that contact is far more important. We encourage all of our teachers to contact the student in a few days after his first absence. This pays real dividends for it lets the person know that he is really missed and that the First Baptist Church in Van Nuys cares about him.

Just a little over a year ago, one Sunday, a new family was absent from our Sunday school and church services. That afternoon the adult teacher of the mother and father called to see if there was illness in the family. Then, the teacher of the junior boy visited in the home to see what he could do about helping if there was a need and the teacher of the primary girl did the same thing. Within just a few hours after these people missed the Sunday school session they had been contacted three times by our people. Is it any wonder that they said, "This church really cares about us." They became faithful supporters of our Sunday school program.

Although not every one of our Sunday school teachers is as faithful as he should be in contacting absentees, we are constantly working on this. We are not going to be content until we have 100 per cent cooperation on the part of our entire faculty.

To multiply by division is not only a sound biological process, it is also a very effective method of developing a Sunday school. This principle is the fourth factor that has contributed much to the growth of our overall teaching program. We do not allow our adult classes to average more than 40 in attendance. When they reach this point we divide them into two classes. We have discovered that by so doing it isn't long until both parts grow to be the same size as the original class and then it becomes necessary to divide again. We follow this same process in all of our departments. We set a maximum goal that the department can achieve. When it achieves that, then it is split into two departments, and on and on the process goes, and in this way, the Sunday school continues to grow.

Before leaving this, let me say one other word about our adult classes. We do not want them to become little churches in themselves. They do not have their own treasuries. We operate on a unified budget. Whatever money is given into the Sunday school class is placed into that budget. We promote our adults on the basis of age, thereby keeping little cliques from forming within the Sunday school and becoming powerful factions that can actually challenge the authority of the church. If you will look at the history of American churches you will discover that many of them have been destroyed because adult Sunday school classes have developed into little churches within the church, competing with the overall program. This cannot happen in our church. By promoting the adults and through multiplying by division, it is impossible for an adult class to become a separate entity.

Shortly after Elmer Towns came out with his book

on the ten largest Sunday schools in America, even though we were in this, we nevertheless were not satisfied with our own program. We wanted to learn as much about what made the other Sunday schools tick as we possibly could. We therefore studied this document. We discovered that one of the contributing factors to the growth of many of the other Sunday schools in the first ten was a bus ministry.

We had twelve buses that we were using in our general program but not as a part of our Sunday school outreach. We immediately decided to emulate the example of these other churches. We called a man to be in charge of our bus ministry. Shortly after he arrived on the scene he trained some of our lay workers to be bus captains. We now have nine bus routes that are picking up both children and adults and bringing them to our Sunday school. This is the fifth factor in contributing to our rapid growth.

We are intending to enlarge this ministry. At the present time we have plans for three more bus routes. When we complete the activating of these routes, we will then be using all of the buses we own. As we expand this program this will necessitate the addition of other buses. We are already taking this into account as we plan our budget for the coming year. I am convinced that this ministry has a tremendous potential for enlisting people in the Sunday school who cannot be reached in any other way. This is due to the fact that so many parents do not care whether their children come to Sunday school or not. If transportation is provided for them so that the parents are not disturbed on Sunday morning, then they are perfectly willing for their boys and girls to come. If the transportation is not provided they will not disturb themselves to transport their offsprings to the Sunday school. Our church in Van Nuys is going to have an ever expanding bus ministry.

The sixth factor contributing to the rapid growth of our Sunday school is that of pastoral support. This in reality is basic to the other five, for it is axiomatic that no program in the church can get off the ground unless it has the support of the pastor. I am vitally concerned about the growth and the development of our teaching program. I will not leave the church after the 11 o'clock service on Sunday until I have gone to the Sunday school office and made a meticulous examination of the record for that day.

If I find a department is down in attendance and as far as I know there is no reasonable explanation for it, I will immediately get in touch with our director of Christian education and ask him to investigate the situation for me. He knows that when I do this, I expect an answer from him within a day or two.

Fortunately, in our church we have a Christian education director who is just as concerned about these matters as I am. Most of the time when I apprise him of a certain department that is down I discover that he knows it and has already investigated the reason for it. Both he and I have a burden to build this Sunday school. He knows he has my unqualified support in what he does and I am sure that if you were to ask him, he would tell you that this means much to him.

Among some of my closest friends in the ministry, there are those who do not have the same attitude toward the Sunday school as I. They take the position, "This is not my bailiwick. I have employed a Christian education director to take care of this matter. I'm not going to check up on him. If the Sunday school does not grow and develop, it is his fault and his problem. That's why we pay him." Where this attitude on the part of the pastor prevails, the Sunday school does not grow. Instead it has a tendency to decline. The Sunday school in the First Baptist Church in Van Nuys has the

100 percent support of its pastor and I am sure that God is blessing it because of this.

Three years ago I had the privilege of delivering a series of messages at the Sunday School Convention in Seattle, Washington. In one of the sessions—an open forum session, I simply told the story of the Van Nuys First Baptist Church and encouraged the ministers in that group to build their churches on the basis of sound preaching and a strong Sunday school program. When the time came for questioning, a young minister stood to his feet. As long as I live I shall never forget the way in which he interrogated me. He said, "My church does not have all the facilities that you have. I have only 100 members. If you were in a situation like this how would you go about developing a strong church? Bear in mind that I don't have money to employ a staff. Whatever is done I have to do it myself. Tell me what would you do in my situation?"

Responding to him, I emphasized the necessity of his studying and preparing good messages, pointing out that the pulpit ministry is pivotal in the building of any church. I then began to talk to him about the developing of his Sunday school and about the fact that church growth comes not only from sound preaching, but also from an effective Christian education program.

I said to him, "If I were in your situation, I would look over my membership to find three people whom I could use as a volunteer staff. I would look for a person who was good at working with adults. I would seek out an individual who had ability in leading young people and then I would look for a third person who knew how to work with children. I am sure that these three people are in your church, and if you would look for them, you would find them. When I found them I would invite them to my house for dinner and I would explain the situation to them.

"Then I would say something like this. 'Even though ours is a small church it is much too large for one man. I need a church staff. Obviously we do not have the budget to employ such a staff. Therefore, I am asking the three of you to become my volunteer church staff. I am going to list you on our stationery as staff members. I will list you this way in our bulletins. I want you to take the adult leadership.' And I would point out the adult leader. 'I want you to take the youth leadership.' And I would point out the youth leader, and, 'I want you to take the children's leadership.' And I would point out the children's leader.

"Then I would say to them, 'It's going to be your responsibility in your area to plan the Sunday school program for Sunday morning and the training program for Sunday evening. It is also your responsibility to recruit the teachers and to see to it that they are properly trained. In addition to this, it is incumbent upon you to stimulate the visitation program.' Then I would ask each of these if he or she was willing to take this responsibility. I would assure each one that I had prayed about it and that I had been led by the Spirit of God to come to him or her with this proposition.

"If each one agreed—and I am sure that nearly any individual in a situation like this who was dedicated to the Lord, would do so—I would then say, 'We are going to have a staff meeting once a week. At this staff meeting, I am going to be a frame of reference for you. If you have any questions about your department and about how to proceed in the various activities within your scope, you ask me and I'll do my best to answer your questions. If I cannot give you the answer immediately, I will find someone who can. At these meetings we are going to set goals for each of our departments and after setting the goals, at the subsequent staff meetings we will check up on ourselves and see how we are measuring up to them. Once we reach a goal in any given department, we'll then set a higher goal and go after that. We will follow this method of operation until our Sunday school becomes strong enough for us to employ full time people to assume the job that you are now going to take.' "

Then I looked at that young preacher and I said, "I would make sure that I kept that staff meeting a sacred hour as far as I was personally concerned. I would let nothing interfere with my meeting with these three people. I would encourage them. I would pray with them and for them, and I would let them know that they were doing a good job for God."

I continued, "If you will follow this plan I will guarantee that your church will grow. Will you try this?" He answered my question in the affirmative.

Two years later, I saw him at another Sunday school convention. He came up to me and said, "You know that plan really worked." And for a minute I didn't know what he was talking about.

I inquired, "What plan?"

He then recalled to my mind what I had said to him in Seattle. He informed me that he went home and immediately began to implement that which I had told him. He said, "I was able to find the three leaders. They agreed to take the jobs. We have met together regularly as a staff and within a short period of time we have doubled our Sunday school and more than doubled our budget. I know that it is not going to be long until we have paid staff members working full time at these jobs that the three volunteers are presently doing." And then looking at me again with a smile on his face, he said, "Thank you for your suggestion. It really worked."

Yes, the building of a great church consists of sound preaching and an ever growing and developing Christian education program. This is the modus operandi that has been followed by the First Baptist Church in Van Nuys, and God has seen fit to place His imprimatur upon us.

EPILOGUE

Now, as I come to the end of this volume, I would like to recommend to my readers that you implement the ten principles it presents as the secret of growth. By so doing, I know that the Holy Spirit will reward you personally, and your church corporately, with success that surpasses your highest dreams. This He has done for us and this He will do for you. May God bless you.